Brahman and the World

Brahman and the World

Ashokanath Bhattacharya Sastri

shakti
publications

Cataloging in Publication Data — DK
[Courtesy: D.K. Agencies (P) Ltd. <docinfo@dkagencies.com>]

Bhattacharya, Ashokanath, author.

Brahman and the world / Ashokanath Bhattacharya.
pages cm
Reprint.
Includes bibliographical references.
ISBN 9788194622109

1. Brahman. 2. Causation. 3. Vedanta. 4. Hindu philosophy.
I. Title.

DDC 294.5921 23

ISBN 978-81-946221-0-9

First published in the *Journal of the Department of Letters*, Calcutta University, vol. XXVIII in 1935, by Calcutta University Press, Calcutta
Retypeset format published in 2020

Published by:
Shakti Publications
797/64 (2nd floor), Lekhu Nagar
Tri nagar, Delhi - 110035
Mob.: 9953680097
e-mail: pub.shakti@gmail.com

Distributed By:
D.K. Printworld (P) Ltd.
Regd. office: *Vedaśrī*, F-395, Sudarshan Park
(Metro Station: Ramesh Nagar), New Delhi - 110015
Phones: (011) 2545 3975, 2546 6019; *Fax*: (011) 2546 5926
e-mail: indology@dkprintworld.com
Website: www.dkprintworld.com

Printed by: Shakti Publications, Delhi

Publisher's Preface

This scholarly work of Pt. Ashokanath Bhattacharya Sastri, Vedantatirtha, was first published in 1935 as an article in the *Journal of the Department of Letters*, vol. XXVIII, of the University of Calcutta. Vedānta, the finest fruit of Indian thought, quintessentially deals with the concept of *Brahman* and Its numerous meanings, nature and relevance to the Indian philosophic systems. Śaṅkara, Bhāskara, Rāmānuja, Madhva and Vallabhācārya, the great protagonists of Advaita, Bhedābheda, Viśiṣṭādvaita, Dvaitādvaita and Śuddhādvaita, respectively, have contemplated a great deal on *Brahman* and its nature and qualities.

The author tries to address a perception among Orientalists that while the Upaniṣads favour the Monistic doctrine, the *Brahmasūtra* of Bādarāyaṇa opposes it on some important points. Therefore this volume studies the philosophies of both Śaṅkara and Bādarāyaṇa in articulating the essential features of *Brahman* and Its association with the real world. In so doing, it discusses the concept of universal cause, the different schools of Vedāntic monism on the doctrine of causation, the doctrine of emancipation based on the theory of causation and the concept of causality of *Brahman* in sister schools of Vedānta.

After offering a detailed Introduction (Chap. 1) to the concept of *Brahman*, Chap. 2 goes on to deal with the concept of universal cause and compares the views of Kapila and Rāmānuja on the doctrine of causation, the differences between the views of Patañjali and Rāmānuja, the theory of the identity of efficient and substantive causes. It also proposes to suggest that causation is an inexplicable appearance not amenable to a logical definition, the Monistic view. It deals with the illusory or apparent cause of *Brahman*, along with a critical estimate of Bhāskara's position, the Buddhist Mādhyamika view and the views of the Grammarians, especially on the philosophical theory of *sphoṭa* and *Śabda-Brahman*, and the Monistic standpoint on the consistency of the doctrine of illusory causation.

In enunciating the position of different schools of Vedāntic Monism on the doctrine of causation, Chap. 3 deliberates on the view of *Padārthatattvanirṇaya*, analyses why twofold *upādāna* is admitted from the point of view of the psychology of perception, deals with the phenomenality of the objective world implied in the subject–object relation in perception, the nature of *avidyā* and its relation to consciousness and the Vivaraṇa view. It houses the interpretation of the Vivaraṇa view and *Saṁkṣepaśārīraka* view, and answers the question as how does the insentience of world come into the philosophical discourse, Vācaspati's view on *māyā* and the insentience of the world together with a critical examination of his position.

Chap. 4 talks about the doctrines of emancipation keeping in mind Appaya Dīkṣita, Rāmānuja and Jaimini and their different views, and explains the different types and stages of emancipation in Vedānta, going by the teachings of Śaṅkara. It further makes a brief mention of the doctrine of causation in the Śruti texts.

The concluding chapter is a study of the concept of causality of *Brahman* in the sister schools of Vedānta. Sureśvara and Vijñānabhikṣu appear to have an analogous view as regards *Brahman* to be the substantive cause. It also provides details of Advaita vs Viśiṣṭādvaita, ideals of Bhāskara vs Śaṅkara; Nimbārka; Bhāskara vs Nimbārka; Nimbārka vs Rāmānuja, Vijñānabhikṣu's position against Śaṅkara and Rāmānuja, Madhva's position and the teachings of the Gauḍīya school and the position of Vallabhācārya on the concept of causality, among some allied topics.

We have adopted a new lay-out with currently prevailing diacritical marks. As value-adds, we have created a brief Bibliography and Index. Hope this book will benefit all who are keen to know about the philosophic teachings of Advaita Vedānta and its preceptors.

Contents

Publisher's Preface v

1. Introduction **1**

A Passing Note on the Identity of the Vṛttikāra 7

2. The Concept of a Universal Cause **10**

Kapila and Rāmānuja about the Doctrine of Causation: A Comparison 10

Patañjali and Rāmānuja 11

The Theory of the Identity of Efficient and Substantive Cause: Supported in the Brahma-Sūtras 12

The Monistic View: Causation Is an Inexplicable Appearance not Amenable to a Logical Definition 14

Brahman: The Illusory or Apparent Cause 15

A Critical Estimate of Bhāskara's Position 18

The Mādhyamika View 22

The View of the Grammarians: Sphoṭa and Brahman 30

Consistency of the Doctrine of Illusory Causation from the Monistic Standpoint 32

3. The Different Schools of Vedāntic Monism on the Doctrine of Causation **35**

The View of the Padārthatattvanirṇaya: Twofold Substantive Cause — Brahman and Māyā 35

Why Twofold Upādāna Is Admitted? The Psychology of Perception 36

The Phenomenality of the Objective World Implied in the Subject–Object Relation in Perception 41

The Nature of Avidyā and Its Relation to Consciousness 45
The Vivaraṇa View: Īśvara (and not Brahman) — the Upādāna 48
Dr Das Gupta's Interpretation of the Vivaraṇa View 48
Saṁkṣepaśārīraka View: Pure Brahman — the Upādāna 50
The Insentience of the World: How Does It Come In? 50
Vācaspati's View 51
Vācaspati Explains the Insentience of the World 51
A Critical Examination of Vācaspati's Position 52
Other Charges against Vācaspati 54
Kalpataru's Support to Vācaspati's Position 60
The View of the Siddhāntamuktāvalī: Brahman — No Upādāna at All: Māyā — the Only Material Cause 62

4. The Doctrines of Emancipation Attendant on the Doctrine of Causation 64

The Question of Individual Release: The Attainment of the State of Īśvara — Appaya Dīkṣita's View 64
Bādarāyaṇa's Views about the Nature of Final Release 67
Difference between Appaya Dīkṣita and Rāmānuja Regarding the Question of Individual Release 69
Which of These Two Views Retains the Spirit of Jaimini? 70
Different Types and Stages of Emancipation in Śaṅkara's School of Vedānta 71
The Doctrine of Causation in the Śruti 75

5. The Conception of the Causality of Brahman in the Sister Schools of Vedānta 81

Advaitins and Vijñānabhikṣu 81
Advaita and Viśiṣṭādvaita 81
The Position of Bhāskara 82
Bhāskara and Śaṅkara 84
The Position of Nimbārka 85

Bhāskara and Nimbārka 87

Nimbārka and Rāmānuja 89

Vijñānabhikṣu's Position 89

Brahman: The Locative Cause of the Universe 90

Śaṅkara, Bhāskara and Bhikṣu 92

An Original Line of Interpretation of the Brahmasūtras: An Attempt at Compromise between Vedānta and Sāṁkhya-Yoga 93

Bhikṣu's Interpretation of the Adhikaraṇas Which Serve as the Support of the Theory of Abhinnanimit-topādāna 97

Madhva's Position 98

The Position of the Gauḍīya School 100

Brahman: The Formative Cause — Gauḍīya View 101

The Position of Vallabha 102

Two Main Divisions of the Commentators of the Brahma-Sūtras Accepting Brahman as the Identity of the Efficient and the Substantive Cause 103

The Particular Sections of the Brahma-Sūtras Dealing with the Doctrine of Causation 105

Bibliography 106

Index 108

1

Introduction

The Vedānta has been rightly called the finest fruit of Indian thought. Indian wisdom has not produced a fairer flower than the Upaniṣads and a finer fruit than the Vedānta philosophy. The Vedānta grows out of the teachings of the Upaniṣads and passes into various systems in the writings of Śaṅkara (*c.* eighth century AD), Bhāskara (*c.* tenth century AD), Rāmānuja[1] (*c.* eleventh century AD), Nimbārka[2] (*c.* eleventh

---

[1] With him may be classed Śrīkaṇṭha (*c.* fourteenth century AD). The only difference between Rāmānuja and Śrīkaṇṭha is that the latter replaces the former's Viṣṇu by Śiva. An earlier commentary of the *Brahma-Sūtras* belonging to the Śaiva Viśiṣṭādvaita school is ascribed to one other Nīlakaṇṭha, who is claimed by his followers to have preceded Śaṅkara even.

[2] With him may be classed the followers of Caitanya (the reputed founder of the Gauḍīya school in Bengal). Baladeva Vidyābhūṣaṇa (eighteenth century AD) wrote his *Govindabhāṣya* on the *Brahma-Sūtras* of Bādarāyaṇa (in which the doctrine of incomprehensible Identity-in-Differnece — Acintyabhedābhedavāda — is established). Some would, however, like to class him with Madhva, and tradition also support this view. But we have reason to believe that the Gauḍīya school of Vaiṣṇavas is more indebted to the school of Nimbārka than to that of Madhva. Jīva Gosvāmin, in his *Ṣaṭsandarbha*, states that the Gauḍīya Vaiṣṇava school is also indebted to some other older commentaries on the *Brahma-Sūtras*, viz., the *Vāsanā Bhāṣya*, the *Hanumad Bhāṣya*, etc. Some seek to identify these two commentaries with the *Bhāskara Bhāṣya* and the *Madhya Bhāṣya* respectively. But nothing definite can be said with regard to this question of identity, unless sufficient data are available.

century AD), Madhva[3] (*c.* thirteenth century AD) Vallabha[4] (*c.* fifteenth century AD) — the great founders of the Advaita, Bhedābheda, Viśiṣṭādvaita, Dvaitādvaita and Śuddhādvaita systems of thought repectively. Most of these orthodox great commentators have written separate commentaries on the Upaniṣads also. Even now, these systems, taken together, represent the beliefs of nearly all thoughtful Hindus and attract the attention of many a great thinker in the East and the West.

The general impression among the present-day Oriental scholar is that though the Upaniṣad texts mainly favour the Monistic doctrine expounded by Śaṅkara, the *Brahma-Sūtras* of Bādarāyaṇa are fundamentally opposed to it on some of the most crucial points.

Almost all the scholiasts, however, are unanimous in their opinion that:

1. the first *five* (or four according to Vallabha) topics (*adhikaraṇas*) of the *Brahma-Sūtras* practically exhaust the entire philosophy discussed in the Vedānta system; and
2. the rest of the *Brahma-Sūtras* seems, to all intents and purposes, to be pre-occupied with an elaboration of the

---

[3] With him may be classed the Pāśupata Śaivas and Vijñānabhikṣu (*c.* sixteenth century AD) who worte his *Vijñānāmṛta Bhāṣya* on the *Brahma-Sūtras*. While Madhva worships Viṣṇu and the Pāśupatas Śiva as the Supreme Deity, Vijñānabhikṣu transcends all sectarian bias and calls the Supreme Being *Īśvara*.

[4] An earlier exponent of Śuddhādvaita school was Viṣṇusvāmin (*c.* twelfth century AD) who is said to have written a commentary on the *Brahma-Sūtras*. But this work is not available at present. According to some, the celebrated commentator Śrīdharasvāmin has very closely followed him in his views. It is true that Śrīdhara refers to Viṣṇusvāmin several times in his commentary on the *Bhāgavata Purāṇa*. But this much is also certain that Vallabha differs from Śrīdhara on some crucial points. The celebrated devotee and poet-philospher Bilvamaṅgala Ṭhākura also belonged to the school of Viṣṇusvāmin — at least so goes the tradition.

main thesis established in the foregoing part by reference to specific doctrines of the Upaniṣads.

It is apparent, therefore, that the work of Bādarāyaṇa is susceptible of two broad divisions — (1) the first part, being a statement of the main thesis, and (2) the second part, forming an amplification and elabortaion of the same subject, however, to occasional introduction of independent topics having only a remote bearing on the main issue. In this matter of division, however, Śaṅkara makes a departure from the usual convention by insisting upon the *Ānandamayādhikaraṇa* to be regarded as an essential part of the corpus of the first division and he has made a vigorous attack upon the previous commentators for relegating it to a position of minor importance as its inclusion in the explanatory section would naturally connote. The real motive underlying the new procedure adopted by Śaṅkara is to emphasise the three essential aspects of features (*svarūpalakṣaṇa*) of *Brahman*, which can be serially arranged in the following order:

1. *The aspect of Being* — unconditional and absolute (*sat*) as set forth in the first four *adhikaraṇas;*
2. *The aspect of Consciousness* — pure and absolute (*cit*) as established in the fifth *adhikaraṇa*; and
3. *The aspect of Bliss* — absolute and unqualified (*ānanda*) as brought out in the sixth *adhikaraṇa.*

It should, however, be noted, in order to avoid the charge of misrepresentation, that in the preface to the *Ānandamayādhikaraṇa*, Śaṅkara openly avows it to form the beginning of the supplementary division and this would seem to contradict the position we have set forth above. But it will be obvious to a careful reader, who will look below the surface, that this statement[5] has been made in deference to the conventional

---

[5] *evam ekam api brahmāpekṣitopādhisambandhaṁ nirastopādhisambandhaṁ copāsyatvena jñeyatvena ca vedānteṣūpadiśyate iti pradarśayituṁ paro* →

interpretation (attributed to a *vṛttikāra* by the commentators of Śaṅkara) and it would be a grave error of judgement to think it to represent the true position of Śaṅkara. The conventional interpretation which Śaṅkara gives in the first instance has been emphatically repudiated by him in the concluding portion of the discourse and this reverses the position he took up in the preface as a tribute to the prevailing convention. So far as Śaṅkara himself is concerned, the topic (*adhikaraṇa*) in question should be undoubtedly taken as an essential part of the main thesis and the philosophical implication, brought out by us, would only bear it out.

From the above discussion it is also evident that long before the days of Śaṅkara there flourished a *vṛttikāra* who had commented on the *Brahma-Sūtras*; and though Śaṅkara had occasions to differ from him on some particular points, this *vṛttikāra* nevertheless was essentially a sturdy Monist in his views. We may be justified, therefore, in believing that Śaṅkara had at least one predecessor in the person of this *vṛttikāra*, who held the Monistic position, though not exactly identical with that of Śaṅkara.

In the first division of the *Brahma-Sūtras*, referred to above, *Brahman* has been defined as the Universal Cause — a rather accidental or functional characterisation; but for an insight into the essential nature of the Reality in and by itself we have to

---

← *grantha ārabhyate.* — Śaṅkara's *Bhāṣya* on the *Brahma-Sūtras* I.1.12, Nirṇayasāgara edn., p. 177.

The above passage may be translated thus:

"From all this it may appear that *the following part of the Śāstra* has a special object of its own, viz., to show that the Vedānta texts teach, on the one hand, *Brahman*, as connected with limiting conditions and forming an object of devotion, and on the other hand, as being free from the connexion with such conditions and constituting an object of knowledge." — Sacred Books of the East Series, vol. XXXIV, p. 64.

deduce it from the import of some aphorisms of Bādarāyaṇa as Absolute Being, Absolute Consciousness, and Absolute Bliss all blended in simple identity.

What sort of cause *Brahman* is, has been definitely mentioned in the second aphorism:

> (*Brahman* is that) from which the origin, etc. (i.e., the origin, subsistence, and dissolution) of this (world proceed).[6]

It is both the efficient (*nimitta*) and the substantive or material (*upādāna*) cause of the phenomenal world. This is apparent from the additive expression '*et cetera*' which stands for preservation (*sthiti*) and universal destruction (*laya*). It should be noted here that in both Vedānta and Sāṁkhya there is no such thing as absolute cessation of existence or being. Destruction, therefore, in the present context should not be interpreted as cessation of existence, but as the passing from the patent, manifested state into the latent, unmanifested state. To be precise, it (destruction) only implies the re-absorption of the effect into its primitive causal state. There is, however, neither loss of being in destruction, nor any addition of the same as the word 'creation' or 'production' would ordinarily imply. Now, if we investigate the nature of the causality of *Brahman*, we shall see that it is both the efficient and the material cause and not alone the efficient cause. Because, destruction in the sense of re-absorption is compatible with *Brahman* being the *Causa Materialis* and not *causa efficiens*. So far as creation and preservation go, they are competent to an efficient cause, no doubt, but they are not repugnant to a material cause. About *Brahman* being the *Causa Efficiens*, the fashioner and preserver of the order, there is no divergence of opinion among the orthodox commentators of the *Brahma-Sūtras*. It is the nature of *Brahman* as material or substantive cause which has been the storm-centre of controversy and polemic. We believe that we have shown

---

[6] *janmādyasya yataḥ* — *BrSū* I.1.2.

that this material or stubstantive causality of *Brahman* cannot be possibly denied without doing violence to the spirit of the text of the aphorisms as well as the philosophy of Vedānta.

Now, the question arises — what sort of material causality (*upādānatā*) is to be ascribed to *Brahman*? Leaving aside for the time being those aphorisms which expressly deal with the nature of the causal relation, to which we shall advert later on, we shall find the answer given in a rather unexpected quarter — in the very first aphorism of the second division:

> The one within (the sun and the eye) (is the highest Lord), on account of His qualities being declared.[7]

We see in this aphorism and the dissertation upon it in the *Śāṅkara Bhāṣya* that the Absolute Self, which is the sole and ultimate cause of all that exists or appears, can easily appropriate to Itself the characteristics of any phenomenon, be it a human being or a divine person; because the cause is the ground of the effect and hence can own up all that belongs to it. But the contrary is not true — the characterstics of the cause cannot be conceived to be appropriated by the effect, which is only a partial manifestation of the same. This, however, is the philosophy of what is technically called the Vivarttavāda — the doctrine of phenomenal or illusory causality. This has been made abundantly clear by Vācaspati in the *Bhāmatī*.[8]

Rāmānuja and others, on the other hand, consider that it is not proper to regard the world as false appearance and so they have concentrate their attacks on the fundamental position of Monistic Vedānta, viz., Vivarttavāda. Thus while the Monists think that *Brahman* (the Absolute) is really destitute of all attributes and limitations and Its association with qualities is due

---

[7] *antas taddharmopadeśāt* — *BrSū* I.1.20.

[8] *Bhāmatī* under *Bhāṣya* on *BrSū* I.2.1, N.S. edn., p. 231. This point will be taken up later on for a detailed discussion of the appropriateness of Vivartta doctrine.

to false imposition, Rāmānuja holds that *Brahman* is qualified (*saguṇa*) in Its essential nature.

We now propose to take up the question of Universal Causation, to examine thoroughly as to how far it is right to regard *Brahman* as the Universal Cause and how far does the *sūtrakāra* himself lend his support to each of the inter-conflicting schools of Vedānta.

A Passing Note on the Identity of the Vṛttikāra

The *vṛttikāra*, referred to in this connection by Śaṅkara, cannot be identical with *vṛttikāra* Bodhāyana, to whom Rāmānuja seeks to affiliate his school,[9] or with Upavarṣa — the pioneer of the Bhedābheda school of which Bhāskara was a champion.[10] Our reason for holding this view is that *prima facie* the interpretation of this topic of discourse (*Ānandamayādhikaraṇa*) as offered by Śaṅkara is held to be a representation of the views of the *vṛttikāra* by Śaṅkara's commentators, notably the author of *Ratnaprabhā*. This is a valuable piece of information, for it gives us a key to the philosophy of the *vṛttikāra*, who is represented to regard the difference between the Absolute and the individual Self as purely fictitious and unreal,[11] which is also the position of Śaṅkara himself. The *vṛttikāra*, who has advocated in no equivocal terms the idea of fictitious difference between *Brahman* and *jīva*, can never be the authority

---

9 *bhagavad-bodhāyanakṛtiṁ vistīrṇāṁ brahmasūtravṛttiṁ pūrvācāryāḥ sañcikṣipuḥ; tanmastānusāreṇa sūtrākṣarāṇi vyākhyāsyante* — *Śrī Bhāṣya*, B.S.S., p. 1.

10 *upavarṣācāryāgamāc ca* — *Bhāskara Bhāṣya*, Chowkhamba S.S., p. 62. *upavarṣācāryasya śāstrasampradāyapravartakasya* — Ibid., p. 134.

11 *īdṛśaṁ ca vijñānātmaparamātmabhedam āśritya 'netaro 'nupapatteḥ' 'bhedavyapadeśāc ca' ityuktam* — *ŚB* on *BrSū* I. 1.17, N.S.S., p. 184.

"With reference to this fictitious difference of the Highest Self and the individual Self, the two last *sūtras* have been propounded."

—S.B.E., vol. XXXIV, p. 70.

of Rāmānuja or Bhāskara who do not admit any such tenets. In the opinion of Mahāmahopādhyāya Anantakṛṣṇa Śāstrī, Bodhāyana and Upavarṣa are two separate persons.[12] But in the *Avantisundarīkathā* ascribed to Daṇḍin,[13] Vyāḍi, Indradatta and Kātyāyana are stated to be the pupils of Upavarṣa who has been named Bodhāyana also. In the *Kathāsaritsāgara* of Somadeva and *Bṛhatkathāmañjarī* of Kṣemendra, however, those very persons and Pāṇini are represented as the students of Varṣa, the elder brother of Upavarṣa. It is further stated in the *Avantisundarīkathā* that this Upavarṣa–Bodhāyana possessed the epithet *kṛtakoṭi*, and is said to have written a gloss (*vṛtti*) on the *Brahma-Sūtras*, which also passed by the same name. Perhaps on the authority of such statements, Vedāntadeśika (*c.* thirteenth century AD) had tried to identify Upavarṣa with Bodhāyana. Mahāmahopādhyāya Prof. Kuppusvāmī Śāstrī has thoroughly discussed the point and has supported the Bodhāyana–Upavarṣa–Vṛttikāra equation.[14] It is disputable, however, whether this mere suggestion by Vedāntadeśika, unsupported as it is by any other older authoritative reference, can be pulled up to the level of an historically acceptable fact. As regards the authenticity of the *Avantisundarīkathā*, it only remains for us to point out that the authority of the work has

---

12 Mm. A.K. Śāstrī, *Vedāntaparibhāṣā*, second edition, pp. 230-31.

13 We are not referring here to the mutilated edition of the *Avantisundarīkathā* already published, but to the MSS, ready for publication under the editorship of Ramakrishna Kavi.

14 *vṛttikārasya bodhāyanasyaiva by upavarṣa iti syān nāma* — Vedānatadeśika, *Tattvaṭīkā*, Brindaban edn., p. 566. Also — "Bodhāyana and Dramiḍācārya, two old Vedāntins presupposed by Ramānuja" — by Mm. Prof. Kuppusvāmī Śāstrī, M.A. — Proceedings and Transactions of the Third Oriental Conference, pp. 465-68. Also Sir S. Radhakrishnan, *Indian Philosophy*, first edition, vol. II, p. 431. The expression *syāt* in Vedāntadeśika's passage denotes mere probability and *not* actual certainty in the matter of the aforesaid identity, which, however, is not unanimously supported.

been questioned by the majority of oriental scholars, and it is extremely difficult to say whether we can derive from the *kathā* any assurance as to identify Upavarṣa with Bodhāyana. In cases of this sort it is probably hopeless *a priori* to expect to find any conclusive evidence. In the absence of a few more significant data, which would enable us to definitely equate Bodhāyana with Upavarṣa and *vr̥ttikāra,* we prefer to leave the question still open.

2

The Concept of a Universal Cause

Kapila and Rāmānuja about the Doctrine of Causation: A Comparison

Rāmānuja holds that *Prakṛti* (the creative principle or matter) is the state of equilibrium of the three elemental qualities or attributes (*guṇas*) — purity or intelligence-stuff (*sattva*), activity (*rajas*) and inertia or matter-stuff (*tamas*). It is a dynamic principle constantly undergoing transformation, and is endowed with creative power (*vikṣepaśakti*) like the non-intelligent Primordial Matter (*Pradhāna*) of the Sāṁkhyas. But unlike the Sāṁkhyas (who advocate the theory of the self-evolution of Matter or *Pradhāna*), Rāmānuja maintains that the evolution of *Prakṛti* is caused and controlled by *Brahman*. *Prakṛti* — the material cause (*upādāna*) of the world — is considered to be the body (*śarīra*), attribute (*viśeṣaṇa*) and mode (*prakāra*) of *Brahman*.[1] And in spite of the natural differences (*svarūpabheda*) between the unspiritual matter-stuff (*bhogya*), individual selves who use that matter-stuff as the object of their spiritual activity (*bhoktṛ*) and *Brahman* — the ultimate guiding and controlling Spirit (*preritṛ*), they are all integrated into the unity of One Concrete Whole. This identity (*aikya*) of the modes (*prakāra*) and the substance (*prakārin*) is

---

[1] "Souls and matter are comprehended within the unity of Lord's essence and are related to the Supreme as attributes to a substance, as parts to a whole, or as body to the soul which animates it. . . . They are real and permanent, though subject to the control of the one *Brahman* in all their modifications and evolutions." — Radhakrishnan, *Ind. Phil.*, vol. I, pp. 684-85.

technically known as the 'inseparable existence' (*apṛthaksiddhi*) — the identity of non-distinction. But like *Brahman*, *Prakṛti* is never regarded as a separate cause, independent of *Brahman*. It is ever under the control of *Brahman* in all its transformations. Thus self-evolution of matter has not got the support of Rāmānuja. Though *Prakṛti*, in the abstract and taken by itself, may be looked upon as the cause of the world, — and *Brahman*, the guiding Principle, can, by the same process, be regarded as the efficient cause of the world, — yet *Brahman* as a Concrete Principle, with *Prakṛti* as its body and Itself as the animating Principle (or *śarīrin* — an embodied Spirit), is regarded as the material cause (*upādāna*) also, as the two can never be viewed as separate principles. Thus according to Rāmānuja, *Brahman* has been technically designated as the efficient and material cause at once (*abhinnanimittopādāna*).

Patañjali and Rāmānuja

The Kāpilas or atheistic Sāṁkhyas do not admit the existence of *Īśvara* (i.e., a personal God), and as such they have postulated the theory of the self-evolution of matter. But the followers of Patañjali who are also called the theistic Sāṁkhyas admitted that *Prakṛti* is the material cause (*upādāna*) of the world, — *Prakṛti*, entirely dependent on and controlled by God.[2]

---

[2] *kecit pradhānaṁ triguṇaṁ kāraṇaṁ pravadanti tu* ।
Īśvaras tad adhiṣṭhātety āhur anye manīṣiṇaḥ ॥

— Quoted in the commentary *Gopālikā* (p. 4) on the *Sphoṭasiddhi* of Maṇḍana. The commentator points out that here the expression *kecit* refers to the Sāṁkhyas, and the expression *anye* refers to the followers of the Yoga philosophy. It should be observed that the theistic position attributed to the followers of Patañjali's Yoga Śāstra here is only one of the possible interpretations and developments. Patañjali's *sūtra* — *kleśakarmavipākāśayair aparāmṛṣṭaḥ puruṣaviśeṣa īśvaraḥ*" (*PāYoSū* I.25) denies God's control over *Prakṛti*. He is only regarded as Omniscient. The same view is also supported in a passage of Śaṅkara's *Bhāṣya* — *tatrāpi śrutivirodhena* →

Thus the Pātañjalas had anticipated the position of the Viśiṣṭādvaita school to a very large extent. The difference between Rāmānuja and the theistic Sāṁkhyas can be summed up in the following proposition:

(a) The Pātañjalas, like the Pāśupata Śaivas, think that *Prakṛti* and *Brahman* have separate existence (*pṛthaksiddha*) and *Brahman* is considered as the efficient cause only and not as the substantive cause also.[3]

(b) Rāmānuja contends that there is inseparable relationship (*apṛthaksiddhi*) between *Prakṛti* and *Brahman*; and *Brahman* is regarded as both the efficient and substantive cause (*abhinnanimittopādāna*).

The Theory of the Identity of Efficient and Substantive Cause: Supported in the Brahma-Sūtras

Rāmānuja deduces his conception of *Brahman* as an efficient and substantive cause in one from the *Brahma-Sūtras* of Bādarāyaṇa. That *Brahman* Itself is the substantive cause (*upādāna*) is supported by the aphorisms:

(i) "(*Brahman* is) the substantive cause also, on account of (this

---

← *pradhānaṁ svatantram eva kāraṇam* . . ." (*ŚB* II.1.3). If we are to follow Patañjali strictly we cannot but admit that the God of Patañjali is rather a figurehead serving only a moral or religious purpose and has nothing to do with cosmic evolution. This is at least the interpretation of Śaṅkara and other Vendāntic writers, and seems to be the position of Vyāsa and Vācaspati. Vijñānabhikṣu, however, gives an interpretation altogether different from that of the previous commentators and the philosophy of Yoga is enunciated as a full-fledged theistic system closely analogous to that of Rāmānuja.

3 The doctrines of the Pāśupata Śaivas have been refuted in the *Brahma-Sūtras* (II.2.37-41). It is a well-known fact that their views were collected in a commentary on the *Brahma-Sūtras* by Śrīkarācārya — one of the leaders of the Ekorāma sect of the Śaiva Liṅgāyat school. The *Śrīkara Bhāṣya* of the Pāśupatas will be published before long from Bangalore.

view) not being in conflict with the promissory statements and the illustrative instance;[4] and

(ii) (*Brahman* is the substantive cause) on account of (the self) making itself; (which is possible) owing to modification;[5]

which declare *Brahman* to be simultaneously the efficient and substantive cause, but not the efficient cause alone as the Pātañjalas and the Pāśupatas believe It to be.

In this connecxion, we should also like to point out that there can be no binding rule that the effect and efficient cause will be of similar nature (*salakṣaṇa*). On the other hand, such a position is generally untenable. We can cite the stock example of the potter (the efficient cause) and the pot (the effect). While the efficient cause is only a conscious subject, the effect is non-conscious. So there can be no harm if these two are essentially of different or dissimilar nature (*vilakṣaṇa*).

In the topic (*adhikaraṇa*),[6] beginning with the aphorism:

(Brahman can) not (be the cause of the world) on account of the difference of character of that, (viz., the world); and its being such, (i.e., different from *Brahman*) (we learn) from Scripture,[7]

the discourse opens with the contention of the rival philosophers — notably the Sāṁkhyas, the Vaiśeṣikas and the Naiyāyikas — "how *Brahman*, which is of a different nature from the world, can possibly be its cause?" And this is met by the *sūtrakāra* himself. He propounds that difference of character (*vilakṣaṇatva*) does not affect the relation of cause and effect, as it is found by uncontradicted experience to obtain between two dissimilar things. The examples of living organisms (such as insects) born from inorganic matter and the growth of hair and nails, inanimate in their nature, from living organisms, bear ample

---

4 *prakṛtiś ca pratijñādṛṣṭāntānuparodhāt* — *BrSū* I.4.23.

5 *ātmakṛteḥ pariṇāmāt* — *BrSū* I.4.26.

6 Technically known as the *na-vilakṣaṇatva adhikaraṇa*.

7 *na vilakṣaṇatvād asya tathātvaṁ ca śabdāt* — *BrSū* II.1.4.

testimony to the heterogeneity of cause and effect. Even if the question be pressed further the fact will remain uncontested that the relation of cause and effect presupposes some amount of heterogeneity.

In this context, we are to interpret the term 'cause' as the substantive cause (*upādāna*) only; because the essential dissimilarity of nature between the efficient cause (*nimitta*) and the effect is almost an axiomatic truth, as pointed out above, and as such requires no such elaborate and knotty discussions as raised by both the parties. The real difficulty lies with the substantive cause alone. And the question whether the effect and the substantive or the material cause are homogeneous or not, is the only problem that is subjected to this elaborate disquisition.[8]

The Monistic View: Causation Is an Inexplicable Appearance not Amenable to a Logical Definition

Let us now examine the position of the Monists. Like Rāmānuja, they also admit *Brahman* to be the identity of the efficient and substantive cause; but they do not accept the interpretation of Rāmānuja's school, which seeks to make out the Absolute as an identity of differences, technically known as the theory of the Qualified Monism (Viśiṣṭādvaitavāda).

The Monists assert that to define the relation of *Brahman* with the world through the help of logical categories is an impossibility; because no relation is possible between the real and the unreal (i.e., phenomenal).[9] If there be any relation at all, it would be indefinable (*anirvacanīya*), i.e., false or phenomenal (*mithyā*). The relation of cause and effect cannot be logically extended to the relation of *Brahman* and the phenomenal world.

---

8 To avoid all these difficulties Madhva has adopted a very ingenious method. According to him the aforesaid *adhikaraṇa* serves only to establish the authoritativeness of the Vedas (*vedaprāmāṇya*).

9 *na hi sadasatoḥ sambandhaḥ* — Śaṅkara's commentary on *Māṇḍūkya Upaniṣad* II.7.

This is the most vital point of difference between the Monists and the followers of other schools of Indian philosophy. Accordingly the Monists have coined their own technical terms to explain their own position.

Brahman: The Illusory or Apparent Cause

The Monists affirm that *Prakr̥ti* or *Māyā* is the material cause which transforms itself into the world (technically called the *pariṇāmopādāna*), while *Brahman* is regarded as the cause which appears to the ignorant as undergoing real modification in the world-process (technically called the *vivartopādāna*). But in reality *Brahman* is only the substratum or fundamental basis (*adhiṣṭhāna*) over which this illusory process takes place, and its appearance to an ignorant mind becomes possible by reason of its being founded upon the real substratum, viz., the Absolute Consciousness.

Thus the Advaitins come to distinguish between two types of causality:

(i) The formative cause (*pariṇāmopādāna*) — the cause which undergoes substantial change while producing the effect. As for example, milk is the formative cause of curd, as the transition into the effect is made possible by a subnstantial change in the nature of the cause — milk.

(ii) The illusory or apparent cause (*vivartopādāna*) — the cause remains absolutely unmodified while the effect is apparently produced from it. In other words, the cause appears as the effect. As for instance, rope may be called the illusory cause of snake, as the appearance of the effect (snake) does not effect the nature of the cause (rope) in any way.[10]

---

[10] *pariṇāmo nāma upādānasamasattākakāryāpattiḥ, vivarto nāma upādānaviṣamasattākakāryāpattiḥ* — *Vedāntaparibhāṣā*, pp. 111-12, Mm. A.K. Śāstrī's edition.

If the effect is of the same order of reality as the cause, it is said to have undergone real transformation, as the change of milk into curd; if, however, the effect (or rather, the appearance of the effect) and the cause are *not* of the same kind of reality; we get a case of illusory appearance, e.g., the rope appearing as the snake.

To sum up, we have seen that the position of the *sūtrakāra* Bādarāyaṇa who maintains the identity of the efficient and material cause of the world-order has received a powerful confirmation and a most rational exposition in the hands of the Monists, we have gone further to demonstrate that the opposite view, i.e., the theory of divergence of efficient and material cause, is logically absurd and contrary to the teaching of the Upaniṣads.

To pursue the Advaita position further, — *Brahman*, as the substratum, is concealed by the veiling power (*āvaraṇa-śakti*) of *māyā*,[11] and is made to appear as the universe by virtue of its projective power (*vikṣepaśakti*). So, really *Brahman* is not the changing material cause (*pariṇāmopādāna*). But that does not debar us from regarding *Brahman* as the apparent cause (*vivartopādāna*). The concept of material cause does not necessarily imply a real process of transformation in the causal stuff and can be applied with equal propriety to the illusory or apparent cause as explained before. The real presupposition of a material cause is that the effect produced derives its existence

---

[11] ". . . *Māyā* is the finitising process belonging to *Brahman*, and has the two properties of *āvaraṇa* or hiding the truth, and *vikṣepa* or misrepresenting it. While the first is a mere negation of Knowledge, the second is positive generation of error. . . . *Māyā* evolves a variety of names and forms, which in their totality is the *jagat* or the universe. It also conceals the eternal *Brahman* under this aggregate of names and forms. *Māyā* has two functions of concealment of the real and the projection of the unreal." — Radhakrishnan, *Ind. Phil.*, vol. II, p. 571.

from the former, and its is absolutely immaterial whether the derivation of existence is real or apparent. The definition of material cause is thus given in the *Siddhāntaleśasaṁgraha* by Appaya Dīkṣita.

> It is that which produces an effect which is non-different from itself.[12]

This identity may either be illusory (*kalpita*) or empirical (*vyāvahārika*). To take the stock example of the shell and silver, the identity between the shell and silver is only illusory, as the silver itself is illusory. In the case of this phenomenal world also, the identity of the world with *Brahman* is equally illusory, subject to the proviso that the illusion in the latter case is of a very long duration and has got more method and consistency in it and so can be easily distinguished from cases of ordinary illusions and dreams. The recognition of this fact has been responsible for the apparent gradation and classification of existence under three heads, viz., the Absolute existence, the empirical existence and the illusory existence. But to be precise and logical, the difference between the two latter kinds of existence is one of degree and not of kind. They are equally false from the standpoint of Absolute Existence. The position has been made clear by Vācaspati in the *Bhāmatī*,[13] where he has fully established the imaginary non-difference between the cause and the effect. The identity is not real. Bhāskara, on the contrary, holds that difference (*bheda*) and non-difference (*abheda*) of the cause and the effect are both equally real.[14]

---

12 *svābhinnakāryajanakatvam* — *SLS*, Benares edn., p. 79.

13 *Bhāmatī* under *ŚB* on *BrSū* II.1.14 — *tad ananyatva adhikaraṇa.*

14 *kāryarūpeṇa nānātvam abhedaḥ kāraṇātmanā* — Bhāskara's commentary, Benares edn., p. 18. The causal state of *Brahman* is unity, while its evolved condition is one of multiplicity. "Things are different in their causal and generic aspects and different as effects and individuals." — Radhakrishnan, *Ind. Phil.*, vol. II, p. 670.

A Critical Estimate of Bhāskara's Position

We feel it imperative that we should enter into the problem of causation and its metaphysical implications before we proceed to other problems. In fact, this is a fundamental problem of all philosophical systems and the Vedānta philosophy in particular has dedicated all its energies to the elucidation of this all-important topic and has raised its superstructure upon the results of the investigation of this problem.

Now, the relation of cause and effect can be either one of identity or of difference, and there is no half-way house between the two, as the two alternatives divide between them the whole realm of reality. Let us examine whether the relation can be one of absolute identity. It is of course undeniable that there is a homogeneity between the cause and the effect and it is this fact which distinguishes a causal relation from a mere accidental sequence. The timber is the cause of the table and not of the curtain because we fail to notice any similarity or homogeneity between them. Even the Vaiśeṣikas, who are empiricists out and out, have not failed to notice this peculiarity. On the contrary, they have postulated it as the universal condition of material causation. Now, the question arises as to what we should understand by this homogeneity or similarity. Is it the identity of nature? No; in that case there can be no distinction between a cause and an effect; the two will be identical and there will remain either the cause or the effect. Then some amount of difference has to be postulated if we are to form a logical estimate of causal relation. But is this difference, then, which we have seen to be indispensable to the conception of causality, one of absolute otherness? No; in that case anything can be the cause of any other thing — the timber will be the cause of the table-cloth, as the two are quite distinct and different. Bhāskara and for that matter all realistic philosophers have found in this position a hard nut to that the relation is neither one of identity nor of difference, but a peculiar one in which the two contradictories are found to have established a family relationship. But this is too much to believe. The position of Bhāskara here pays but scant regard to the demand of logical consistency and violates the fundamental laws of thought, viz., the law of Identity and the law of Excluded Middle. A can be A, or not-A, but not both or neither. If you insist that is found to be so in experience and that experience is the ultimate court of appeal in such a dispute, we shall only observe that uncritical experience, without being subjected to a logical examination, is an unsafe and unreliable guide. We see the moon to be of the size of a small silver plate, and there is no occasion for its being invalidated another experience, but this does not warrant the validity of the experience in question. Even the rabid empiricist, who does not hesitate to immolate our local sense at the altar of the God of Experience, will demur to accept the verdict of experience in this instance as true and final. And why do you discredit the verdict, we ask with all humility. Certainly you must admit,—because it militates against reason. So experience cannot be believed to be antagonistic to reason, and where there is this apparent contradiction, we must conclude that there is something rotten in experience.

Now, to revert to our old problem — the problem of causation. We have seen that the relation is a peculiar one and is inconceivable without reference to identity and difference — both at the same time. But identity and difference are contradictory and so cannot be predicated of the same thing. Bhāskara calls upon us to accept this position on the strength of experience, but we have seen that this experience may be unreliable and it *is* so when it is opposed to reason and infringes the fundamental laws of thought. And so long as our logical sense refuses to be coaxed or coerced into the implicit acceptance of a contradictory proposition, and so long as we cannot change the constitution of our minds, we cannot accept the explanation of Bhāskara, which is only a dodge and a subterfuge to evade the logical difficulty. So identity and difference cannot both be true, but it is undeniable that they are found to be the essential characteristics of a causal relation. Without identity the causal relation cannot be distinguished from cases of mechanical or accidental sequence and without the aspect of difference the causal relation becomes an impossible phenomenon. The cause and the effect must be different and distinct; otherwise there will be either the cause or the effect but not both, which is, however, seen to be the very connotation of causal relation. Yes, this is the plain testimony of experience no doubt, but that does not invest it with a character of sanctity. An absurd position cannot be accepted even on the testimony of the Vedas. What would be the legitimate procedure in charactersising this relation? The followers of Śaṅkara have not failed to rise to the height of their conviction and they declare that it is an absurdity — an illusory appearance like that of the silver on the shell and is the product of the same illusive *māyā* which produces the whole show of the world-process. The identity and the difference both are false and inexplicable by logic. The fact is there is no doubt, and we must bow to the inevitable and cannot deny its existence; but with this difference from Bhāskara and his ilk that we cannot accept it to be absolute truth.

We have seen that the position of Bhāskara, who postulates a real development and a real transformation in the nature of the Absolute, is fraught with self-contradiction and so cannot commend itself to any sane man, whose logical sense has not been drugged and dulled by the illogical vagaries of the so-called philosophers. But are we then to jump to the conclusion of the Nihilist that nothing exists and the whole world, subjective and objective, is but an empty show? No; such is not the position of the Vedāntic Monists and they have been far too sane and far too critical to accept this to be the case. The answer to this question has been sought and found in the analysis of any case of ordinary error and illusion. Take the notorious instance of shell-silver. The silver, declare the Vedāntic Monists, is an empty appearance no doubt, but the show is not all. It will be a height of logical inaptitude to think that the appearance is the whole of it. If we probe the situation deeper, we cannot fail to see that the appearance arises over a basic reality — even the simulation of existence is possible if there is behind it a true reality. So the world is not an unmitigated illusion, but an illusion which is founded upon a true reality, viz., the Absolute Consciousness. Śaṅkara has very pertinently observed that all errors are a case of confusion of real and unreal — a pairing together of a truth and a falsehood. This is the fundamental difference from the Mādhyamikas, at least a class of them whose views we find to be expounded in the *Mādhyamika-Kārikās* of Nāgārjuna. We see in the world that there is continual change. But this change presupposes some identity which is to change. So identity (*abheda*) and difference (*bheda*) — continuity and change — are the fundamental keynotes of all experienced reality. But we have seen that both cannot be true at the same time, and if we are confronted with the alternative of accepting one and rejecting the other, we must reject the aspect of difference as unreal appearance, dancing upon the basic foundation of unity or non-difference; because difference cannot arise except on the foundation of two units, which are in their nature simple unities. If one of the two units be absent, the concept of difference becomes impossible, as each of the units constitutes its foundation and pivot; and if the foundation be lacking, how can it subsist? But the case of unity is quite different. It is perceived in and by itself and without any reference to any other unity. Difference, however, is contingent upon unity and without unity its existence is inconceivable. And if one of them is to be discarded, we must give up the aspect of difference as false superimposition and accept the factor of unity as the basic reality; because unity is the presupposition of difference and even if difference be accepted to be the final truth, unity will have to be accepted, as difference without unity as its basic support is a chimera. So between identity and difference we must perforce accept identity as the reality, since identity cannot be rejected as it is the constitutive factor and is the *raison d'être* even of difference.

Thus the theory of simultaneous difference and non-difference of Bhāskara has been very severely criticised by Vācaspati in the *Bhāmatī* (under *ŚB* on *BrSū* II 1.14) by affirming the unreality of difference and the reality of non-difference, basing his arguments on the doctrine of the three different degrees and kinds of reality — the illusory existence (*prātibhāsika-sattā*), the phenomenal existence (*vyāvahārika-sattā*) and the Ultimate Reality (*pāramārthika-sattā*) — popularly known as the doctrine of three types of reality (*sattātraividhya-vāda*). Vācaspati challenges with unimpeachable logic the view of Bhāskara who supports the doctrine of the real evolution of the non-intelligent aspect of *Brahman*.[15]

The point, however, is this: as the apparent cause (*vivartopādāna*) also is identical with the effect, the use of the term *prakṛti* in the aphorism — *prakṛtiś ca . . .* (I.4.23), has its own justification even from the standpoint of those that regard *Brahman* as the illusory cause only.

The Mādhyamika View

The Mādhyamika school of Buddhists holds almost a similar position. The *śūnya* of the Mādhyamikas is *not* an absolute void, emptiness, non-being, non-entity or non-existence as we are prompted to think of it at the very first sight. It has been described in the *Mādhyamika-Kārikās* of Nāgārjuna as something which is neither real or existent, nor unreal or non-existent, nor

---

15 *bhāskarīyās tu cidacidaṁśavibhaktaṁ brahmadravyam acidaṁśena vikriyate* । — *Sarvārthasiddhi* III.27

both, nor neither.[16] Professors Th. Stcherbatsky and Yamakami Sogen, following the traditional exposition prevalent in China and Japan, assert that it is the fifth kind of existence — "the unique, undefinable (*anirvacanīya*) Essence of Being, the One-without-a-Second" (Stcherbatsky).

In the Bhāvādvaita doctrine,[17] ascribed to the celebrated Monist teacher Avimuktātma-Bhagavān (*c.* ninth century AD) — the author of *Iṣṭasiddhi*,[18] the destruction or removal of nescience (*avidyā-nivṛtti*) at the time of Final Release (*mokṣa*) is described to be of a similar type.[19] Like the *śūnya* of the Mādhyamikas,

---

[16] *śūnyam iti na vaktavyam aśūnyam iti vā bhavet* ।
ubhayaṁ nobhayaṁ ceti . . . . ॥
— *Mādhyamikaśāstra*, p. 94

Cf. . . . . *tattvaṁ sadasadubhayānubhyātmakacatuṣkoṭivinirmuktaṁ śūnyam eva*. — *Sarvadarśanasaṁgraha*, A.S.S. edn., p. 11.

[17] Referred to in the *Gauḍabrahmānandī* (*Laghucandrikā*) on *Advaitasiddhi*, N.S. edn., p. 885. Of course, Madhusūdana or Brahmānanda does not accept this view —

ye tu pañcamaprakārādipakṣāḥ, te tu mandabuddhivyutpādanārthā iti.
— *Advaitasiddhi*, N.S. edn., p. 885

[18] The general idea is that the Bhāvādvaita doctrine belongs to Maṇḍana Miśra — the author of *Brahmasiddhi*. But the quotations found in the *Advaita-brahmasiddhi* and *Siddhāntaleśasaṁgraha* prove the fact to be otherwise. *Advaitabrahmassidhi* attributes the doctrine to the author of *Iṣṭasiddhi* and others. *Siddhāntaleśasaṁgraha*, on the other hand, expressly states this doctrine to belong to Ānandabodhācārya. *Citsukhī* too maintains that this view does not belong to *iṣṭasiddhikāra* (vide below).

[19] *uktaprakāracatuṣṭayottirṇapañcamaprakāra iti* . . . *iṣṭasiddhikārādayaḥ*. — *Advaitabrahmasiddhi*, Bib. Ind., pp. 201-02. *uktaprakāracatuṣṭayottīrṇā pañcamaprakārety ānandabodhācāryāḥ*. — *SLS*, Benares edn., p. 500. Appaya Dīkṣita says that according to Maṇḍana, *avidya-nivṛtti* is denial with *Ātman* — *keyam avidyā-nivṛttiḥ? ātmaiveti brahmasiddhikārāḥ*. — *SLS*, pp. 497-98. The actual quotation from Maṇḍana's *Brahmasiddhi* is, however, found in *Citsukhī*, in which *ajñāna-nivṛtti* is identified with *vidyā* or *brahma-jñāna* — *Vidyaiva* →

it is beyond the limits of all categorical assertion and is of the fifth kind. While according to the interpretation of Professors Stcherbatsky and Yamakami Sogen, the Mādhyamikas posit the *śūnya* (the principle of Relativity — some sort of unrestricted hyper-existence) as the Essence of this universe (if any essence could be attributed at all), the followers of the Bhāvādvaita doctrine assert that the destruction of ignorance (which is also a fifth kind of prediction like the *Śūnya*)[20] can never be the character of the world. So a distinct category of existence which *appears* as the cause, has to be postulated. This is *Brahman*.[21]

← *vādvayā śāntā tadastamaya ucyate*. — *Cit.*, N.S. edn., p. 381. *Citsukhī*, following Maṇḍana and *iṣṭasiddhikāra*, identifies *ajñāna-nivṛtti* with *Ātman* when its true nature is known to the enlightened person — *tasmād utpannātmavijñānasya jñāta ātmaiva savilāsājñānanivṛttir iti sthitam*. — Ibid., p. 383. According to *Citsukhī*'s interpretation, *iṣṭasiddhikāra* does not hold the view that *ajñāna-nivṛtti* is of the fifth type; on the other hand, his view is that *ajñāna-nivṛtti* is equivalent to the object known or the knowledge of the object. *Citsukhī* gives the actual quotation from *Iṣṭasiddhi* — *jñāto'rthas tajjñaptir vā jñānahānir itīṣṭasiddhikārair abhidhānāt*. — Ibid., p. 381. Madhusūdana Sarasvatī holds the same view as that of *Citsukhī* — *caramavṛtyupalakṣitasyātmano 'jñānahānirūpatvāt* — *Advaitasiddhi*, N.S. edn., p. 884.

20 As we have already seen that celebrated teachers like Maṇḍana Miśra, Citsukhācārya, Madhusūdana Sarasvatī and a host of others unanimously reject this position. In their opinion, *Ātman* (i.e., *Brahman*) with its true nature known, or *Vidyā* (i.e., the Supreme Knowledge of *Brahman*) is identical with the removal of nescience (*avidyā-nivṛtti*). Though the author of *Advaita-brahmasiddhi* ascribes this peculiar doctrine to the author of *Iṣṭasiddhi*, the quotation from *Citsukhī* proves the fact to be otherwise. In the absence of a few more significant data, we should like to leave the question open for the present. There is yet a third view, according to which it is indefinable (*anirvācyā*) or false (*mithyā*) like *avidyā*.

21 *Brahman* also is called *Śūnya* in *Yogasvarodaya Brāhmaṇa* and *Mahopaniṣad* — *śūnyaṁ saccidānandaṁ niḥśabdabrahmaśabditam*.

We feel, we should utter one word of caution here. So far as Nāgārjuna is concerned, it is difficult to deduce any positivistic Absolutism from his *kārikās*. He, on the contrary, emphatically repudiates even the remotest suggestion of an eternal entitative category and loses all patience with those who would hypostatise the *śūnyatā* as an ultimate existence. In fact, all the predicates used with reference to *śūnyatā* are of a purely negative character and can be used with equal facility of both Absolute Being and Absolute Non-Being. It is exceedingly hazardous, therefore, to postulate an Absolute of the nature of *Brahman* (which is undoubtedly Unrestricted Existence) on the statements of Nāgārjuna, which are purely of a non-committal character.

The difference between the *Śūnya* of the Mādhyamikas and the *Brahman* of the Advaitins, as interpreted by the two Russian and Japanese savants, lies in the fact that the *śūnya* is mere unrestricted existence — 'the Essence of Being',[22] while *Brahman* is Absolute Being-Consciousness-Bliss (*Saccidānanda*). It is problematic whether this unrestricted existence is of the nature of Consciousness or Self-consciousness, so to say.

The line of demarcation that has been drawn in the foregoing

---

22 Prof. Stcherbatsky calls it so; the full quotation is given above. Vide *The Conception of Buddhist Nirvāṇa*, Th. Stcherbatsky, Ph.D., pp. 47-48. "The ideal state of absolute unrestrictedness. . . . " — Yamakami Sogen, *Systems of Buddhistic Thought*, p. 202. ". . . Unconditional, independent and absolutely unrestricted. . . . " — Ibid., p. 209. It would not be out of place to point out here that one school of Mādhyamikas, however, attributes the aspect of consciousness also to the *Śūnya* — *kevalāṁ saṁvidaṁ svasthāṁ manyante madhyamāḥ punaḥ*. — *Sarvadarśanasaṁgraha*, A.S.S., p. 19, quoted from *Vivekavilāsa* VIII.273. *Kecit tu mādhyamikāḥ svasthaṁ jñānam āhuḥ — manyante bata madhyamāḥ kṛtadhiyaḥ svasthāṁ parāṁ saṁvidam*. — *Ṣaḍdarśanasamuccaya of Haribhadra with Guṇaratna's Tarkarahasyadīpikā*, p. 47. The same quotation is found verbatim in the *Prameyaratnakośa of Candraprabhasūri*, p. 73.

paragraph between the Śūnyavāda and the Monism of Śaṅkara, is founded upon the exposition of Professors Stcherbatsky and Yamakami Sogen. We have not given our independent judgement about the final philosophical position, which we are tempted to believe, is rather pure negativism. Our reason for this difference of view lies in this that Nāgārjuna has not himself left any statement which can be interpreted as an evidence of a positive ontological principle. And if we are to believe Candrakīrti to have interpreted the position of Nāgārjuna correctly, we also cannot refuse to arrive at the conclusion that Nāgārjuna promulgated a philosophy of absolute negativism. Moreover, the interpretation that has been put upon the philosophy of Śūnyavāda in the orthodox school of the brāhmaṇas bears out the position indicated here. Śaṅkarācārya, Udayana, Vācaspati, Śrīharṣa, Vidyāraṇya and a host of other Brāhmanical writers have all along believed and represented the philosophy of Śūnyavāda as a denial of all ultimate existence, both subjective and objective, conscious and unconscious alike.

Śrīharṣa successfully proved that the whole objective world was a mysterious appearance of which no logical explanation was possible, and this is known as 'Anirvacanīyavāda' — the impossibility of logical explanation. The world-appearance, he argues, cannot be explained in terms either of aught or of naught. If the world were a pure non-entity, its appearance to a mind could not be explained, as a non-entity like a hare's horn or a barren women's son was never seen to appear to a consciousness. Nor can it be regarded as a real entity, as it is seen to be sublated by subsequent experience just like the shell-silver. The silver is a non-entity no doubt, but subject to this important qualification that though a non-entity in and by itself, it somehow appears, which distinguishes it from pure non-entity (*alīka*) like a barren women's son. So a new term had to be coined to describe these facts, viz., *mithyātva* (or falsity) as opposed to pure non-entities, which are never amenable to direct perception.[23] Śrīharṣa is accused by a hypothetical or an actual opponent of preaching a philosophy of absolute negativism for his explaining away the whole world as an illogical appearance and he was ridiculed as an advocate of absolute nihilism like the Mādhyamikas. He explains the fundamental difference of Vedāntic Absolutism from the Śūnyavāda in the following terms:

> The Buddhist nihilist, he observes, believes the whole order of existence including consciousness as an irrational appearance, but the Vedāntist maintains that Consciousness as an ultimate fact cannot be denied without self-contradiction.[24]

Ānandapūrṇa observes that the Buddhist regards consciousness as always relative to an object and the two are inseparable and indistinguishable.[25] In fact, the Buddhist here takes up the position of the subjective idealist who holds that awareness and its object are identical and argues that when the object of awareness is an unreal fiction, the awareness, too, cannot but be unreal, as two identical things cannot have opposed characteristics. The Vedāntist here joins issue and points out that the relation of object and awareness is not one of real identity, but of illusory identity, or rather one that cannot be described in terms of identity or of difference alike. The relation is a false relation and so the identity also is false. It would be height

---

23 *yadasad bhāsamānaṁ tan mithyā. . . .* — *Pañcadaśī*, II.70

24 *saugatabrahmavādinor ayaṁ viśeṣo yad ādimaḥ sarvam evānirvacanīyaṁ varṇayati . . . . vijñānavyatiriktaṁ punar idaṁ viśvaṁ sadasadbhyāṁ vilakṣaṇaṁ brahmavādinaḥ saṅgirante. . . .* — Śrīharṣa, *Khaṇḍanakhaṇḍakhādya*, Chowkhamba S.S., p. 125.

25 *saṁvedanaṁ ca saṁvedyavyatirekeṇa nopalabhyate, ato na svatantram asti — ityādiyauktikabuddhyā vivicyamānānāṁ jñānānāṁ jñeyānāṁ ca svarūpaṁ nāvagamyate. jñeyena jñānasya nirūpaṇāt, jñānena ca jñeyasya nirūpaṇāt naikam api paramārtham* — Ānandapūrṇa, *Vidyāsāgarī*, Chow. S.S., p. 126.

of unreason to argue into the falsity of Consciousness on the basis of this false identity. Vidyāraṇya has made a very strong case in favour of the eternal existence of Consciousness as an ultimate fact. You can deny anything, says Vidyāraṇya, but not Consciousness, because a successful denial of Consciousness is itself possible if you are conscious of it. So Consciousness is ultimately undeniable.[26]

The Ultimate Reality is held to be of the nature of Absolute Existence, Absolute Consciousness and Absolute Bliss or Joy. It may be argued that this Ultimate Reality may be mere existence and not Consciousness. But this will lead to an absurdity. An existence which is not Consciousness has no evidence in its favour. Consciousness is independent of foreign evidence, because it is self-revealing (*svaprakāśa*). If the Ultimate Existence be dependent upon a Consciousness different from itself, it would be found to be on the level of the material world, which Vedānta proves to be an irrational and illogical appearance, with no logical validity in it. So the Ultimate Reality cannot be unconscious. Now, it may be further argued, — 'let it be Consciousness alone, why do you insist that it must be an existence?' No; if Consciousness is not an existence, it will be non-existence and hence mere void (*śūnya*). So the Ultimate Reality must be Existence and Consciousness both at once. And the nature of Bliss is a matter of direct experience — after all it is the dearest of all, the only thing a man cares to preserve; and all other things are prized or hated only as they are supposed to be serviceable or hostile to one's own Self — which is Consciousness and existent Consciousness at that. We see that the exposition of the Ultimate Category as an unrestricted existence alone is not logically sound, as an Ultimate Existence is self-contradictory unless it is held to be identical with Consciousness. We find, however, in some Jaina works (referred

---

[26] *sarvabādhe na kiñcic ced yan na kiñcit tad eva tat* ।
bhāṣā evātra bhidyante nirbādhaṁ tāvad asti hi ॥ — *Pañ*. II.311.

to before) that a class of Mādhyamikas believed the Ultimate Reality to be a self-existent Consciousness and this position is undoubtedly sounder than that of the Russian and the Japanese savants. But this, too, would be an imperfect reality wihout the element of joy in it and Vedānta supplies the lacuna. It is a pity that the Absolute of Vedānta has been grossly misunderstood in some quarters and people have failed to note the philosophical importance of the aspect of *ānanda* (Bliss or Joy). But for this the existence of the world would be intolerable. Nay, the Absolute would be the most miserable Being, imprisoned within Its own existence, which has, however, no charm for It. A feelingless and unconscious existence would be perferable to this. So Vedānta declares that It is full in Itself — full of Joy, nay, Fullness of Joy — the plenum of Existence, Consciousness and Joy. Without Joy, It would fall short of Fullness and hence would not be the Absolute.

In spite of these differences, the Bauddha view, however, seems to approach very near the Advaita position. For even in this Bauddha view, this world of experience is said to be of a purely illusory nature (*sāṁvr̥ta*). Nāgārjuna, the author of the *Mādhyamika-Kārikās*, affirms that even Lord Buddha himself did recognise two different kinds of truth —

(a) Transcendent, absolute truth (*paramārtha satya*), and

(b) relative, conditional, conventional, empirical or pragmatic truth (*sāṁvr̥ta satya*).

The Advaitins, too, urge the phenomenality of the world at every step in their arguments. Had the world been a transformation of a real cause, the position of the Mādhyamikas would have been untenable. For then the product also would have been taken as real and not empirical. The drift of our discussion only points out that the *vivartta* theory is forced upon the Mādhyamikas, if only *Śūnya* is regarded as conscious and joyful also. For it is Consciousness alone that can be concealed by the veiling power of nescience.[27] Perhaps with this object in view, one school of the Mādhyamikas has described the *Śūnya* as of the nature of Pure Consciousness as already referred to in the preceding pages.

The View of the Grammarians: Sphoṭa and Brahman

The doctrine of illusory or apparent creation is found to be fully discussed in the *Vākyapadīya* of Bhartṛhari, the celebrated exponent of the Pāṇinian school of Grammarians. These Grammarians generally advocate the theory of *sphoṭa* or super-subtle Word-Essence. The indeterminate and indivisible essence of Word is the *sphoṭa*. *Sphoṭa* (i.e., *śabda* in its ultimate and unmanifested essence) appears to be the cause of the material world (*artha*), from which it is non-different; and out of it the entire world-process evolves.[28] In the opinion of the Grammarians, *sphoṭa* appears to be the cause of the world. It is super-subtle like the *Brahman* of the Monists; and so it cannot possibly transform itself into the form of this gross world. It is only taken to appear as the product. So the position of the Grammarians appears to be similar to that of the Vedāntic Monists, so far as the question of causation is concerned and the systems also seem to agree in their respective conceptions of *Brahman* and *sphoṭa* as spiritual in nature. Bhartṛhari and his commentators emphasise the spiritual nature of *sphoṭa*, which is also described as *Brahman*, eternal and imperishable. The creation of the multiform world takes place by a process of differentiation in the indivisible essence of *Śabda-Brahman* into a word and a sense — though the two are one in nature. The

---

27 This point will be taken up for a detailed discussion in a subsequent work, in connection with the seven antinomies (*anupapattis*) put forward by Rāmānuja against the veiling ignorance.

28 *anādinidhanaṁ brahma śabdatattvaṁ yad akṣaram* ।
vivartate 'rthabhāvena prakriyā jagato yataḥ ॥ — *Vākyapadīya*, I.1

By using the expression *vivartate*, Bhartṛhari explicitly states that matter is the *vivartta* of the super-subtle Word-Essence.

differentiation is rather illusory so far as the identity of *Brahman* is concerned.[29]

In introducing his philosophy of *sphoṭa*, Bhartṛhari has described it as existent with the help of the expression — "without origin and annihilation", and as omnipresent by the term *brahma*.[30] But as we have already stated above, the theory of illusory or apparent causation (Vivarttavāda) is possible only if the veiling power of nescience is accepted. In the Monistic system, *Brahman*, though non-related, appears to be so by the operation of the veiling power of *avidyā*, and thereby appears as the world. Again, in the opinion of the Monists, Consciousness alone can be covered up by nescience. If the *sphoṭa*, on the other hand, be unconscious, it cannot be regarded as concealed and cannot, therefore, be regarded as only appearing as matter in the manner already explained. Mādhava has also regarded *sphoṭa* as conscious and spiritual in nature, and the universe as an illusory appearance superimposed on it. If that be the real position of the Grammarians, there seems to be very little difference between Advaitavāda and Śabdabrahmavāda. Jayanta, too, sees no difference, if the *sphoṭa*, he observes, be looked upon as a conscious principle, as found in the Upaniṣads.[31]

If the interpretation of the later commentators can be accepted as truly representing the original philosophy of Bhartṛhari, then also we do not find any material difference between the two positions — Vedāntic Monism and that of the Grammarians. The question is raised, — how can these

---

29 . . . *nirvibhāgaḥ śabdārthamayo bodhasvabhāvaḥ śabdaḥ sphoṭalakṣaṇa eva vākyam.* — Puṇyarāja's commentary on the *Vākyapadīya*, p. 71.

30 *anādinidhanapadaniveditā vastusattā nityatvaṁ brahmapadapratipāditaṁ ca vyāpitvaṁ.* — *Nyāyamañjarī*, V.S.S., p. 531.

31 *acetanatvena śabdasya īśvarasyeva sraṣṭṛtvānupapatteḥ* — *Nyāyamañjarī*, Ibid., p. 535. Also — *atha vijñānam ānandaṁ brahmety āgamavacanam anusaratā vibhutvam iva cetanatvam api śabdabrahmaṇo varṇyate, tarhi īśvarasyaiva śabdabrahmeti nāma kṛtaṁ syāt. . . .* — Ibid., pp. 535-36.

be related to Pure Consciousness (which *Śabda-Brahman* is by Itself) — a second principle, viz., ignorance? The answer is given — yes; there can be no real relation, but one is assumed on the evidence of ego-consciousness and the like to function upon Consciousness. And in reality the cause of all effects is *avidyā* or ignorance alone.[32]

Consistency of the Doctrine of Illusory Causation from the Monistic Standpoint

The fundamental principle of homogeneity of the cause and the effect on which the Sāṁkhya system rests may be set forth as a stumbling block in the way of the Monists who advocate the doctrine of illusory or apparent causation, as in the way of those who hold the theory of the real transformation of *Brahman* (Brahmapariṇāmavāda). In the topic of the *Brahma-Sūtras*, discussing the homogeneity of the cause and the effect,[33] the Sāṁkhyas urge that *Brahman* cannot be the cause of the world, since the two are of different nature — the cause being conscious, the effect can never be non-conscious. The argument is directed against those who assert that in the process of creation *Brahman* transforms Itself into the form of the world; and hence it might seem that the Monists, too, cannot possibly hope to escape the charge by merely calling *Brahman* the apparent cause. Because in the Vivarttavāda also, as in the Pariṇāmavāda, some similarity of nature is essential. We may cite, for example, a concrete case of appearance. It is seen that the shell invariably appears as silver, but never as charcoal (*iṅgāla*), as there is some similarity between the shell and the silver, but none between the former and charcoal. So similarity of nature is the determining condition of all causality — real or illusory.

But between Consciousness and the material world there

---

32 *Vaiyākaraṇasiddhāntamañjūṣā* of Nāgeśa Bhaṭṭa with the commentary *Kuñjikā* by Durbalācārya, Chow. S.S., p. 393.

33 *na-vilakṣaṇatva adhikaraṇa* — *BrSū* II.1.4-11.

is absolutely no similarity. If we go deeper into the question, we must see that similarity is unpredictable of the Absolute Consciousness, which has neither qualities nor parts in It; but similarity is based upon a large number of common qualities or of parts. So the world cannot be regarded as illusory superimposition also (much less a real transformation) on indivisible Pure Consciousness, and this reduces creation or false appearance of the world to an impossibility. It might be urged that similarity is not the universal condition of false appearance (*adhyāsa*); as the crystal vase is seen to appear as red though there is no similarity between a red and a white thing. But this is irrelevant. The superimposition of the red colour is due to the presence of a scarlet flower and is conditional (*sopādhika*) upon it. But no such condition can be pointed out in the case of the appearance of the world on the substratum of Pure Consciousness. The superimposition of such concepts, as agency (*kartṛtva*) and the like, may be explained by reference to the presence of egohood (*ahaṁkāra*) as a condition, but so far as the whole world and the physical organism are concerned, their superimposition is not contingent on such condition. The Vedāntist replies that the contention of the Sāṁkhyas is baseless. Similarity is not the universal condition of even unconditional (*nirupādhika*) superimposition. The snake is perceived to have a fragrance like that of the *ketakī* flower. Here the similarity of smell is a felt fact, but it cannot be explained on the basis of common qualities or of parts. So similarity may exist between the material world and the impartite and qualityless Consciousness. We, however, make no fetish of similarity. Similarity is one of the likely causes even of unconditional superimposition. The conch-shell is perceived to be yellow. The yellowness does not belong to the conch-shell itself, and yet it appears over it, though similarity cannot be trotted out as explanation. The cause of this false appearance is the presence of jaundice in the percipient. So we see that either similarity or the presence of a sufficient cause is necessary to make the emergence of false appearance possible, and here in the case of *Brahman* and the world, the presence of *avidyā* as the cause of such appearance is not lacking; — and this explains the apparent anomaly raised by the Sāṁkhyas. We may quote here Vācaspati also in support of the position which we have adopted from the *Vivaraṇa* and the *Tattvadīpana*.[34] Vācaspati says:

> The whole world is a false appearance on the unchangeable Absolute Consciousness due to the working of beginningless false tendencies and impressions and is independent of similarity.[35]

So we see that the two important school of Śāṅkara Vedānta — *Vivaraṇa* and *Bhāmatī* — are unanimous in this respect and that they have exposed the fallacy of the Sāṁkhyas as due to partial observation and unwarranted generalisation.

Hence the proposition — '*Brahman* is the *Prakṛti* (substantive cause) of the material world' — may be interpreted to show that *Brahman* is to be regarded as manifested in the form of the universe, — that *Brahman* appears as the world, in the sense explained above. The expression *prakṛti* would have to be taken in the sense of the apparent or illusory cause (*vivartopādāna*), and not as the really transforming or formative cause (*pariṇāmopādāna*). *Brahman* is thus the apparent cause; since It is hidden by *Māyā* which, again, is generally recognised by the Monists as really changing into the manifested universe.

The different schools of Advaita thinkers hold diverse opinions on this point. It is, therefore, necessary to examine the views of some of the leading schools in detail.

---

34 *Vivaraṇa*, V.S.S., pp. 9-10, and *Vivaraṇaprameyasaṁgraha*, V.S.S., p. 13, and *Tattvadīpana*, p. 81, Mm. A.K. Śāstrī's edn.

35 *vivartas tu prapañco 'yaṁ brahmaṇo'pariṇāminaḥ* ।
anādivāsanodbhūto na sārūpyam apekṣate ॥

Bhāmatī under *BrSū* I.2.21, N.S. edn., p. 257. Also vide *Sarvadarśanasaṁgraha*, A.S.S., pp. 144-45.

3

The Different Schools of Vedāntic Monism on the Doctrine of Causation

The View of the Padārthatattvanirṇaya: Twofold Substantive Cause — Brahman and Māyā

The author of the *Padārthatattvanirṇaya* believes that *Brahman* and *Māyā* are both material causes of the universe, since the diverse characteristics of both *Brahman* and *Māyā* (i.e., both existence and insentience) can be predicated of the material world. The world is non-different from *Brahman*, which alone is the true Being appears to undergo transformation. The reality that is *Brahman* is seen to underlie this material world also. For, in all our worldly experiences, we call it existent (*sat*). Again, this universe is said to be non-different from *Māya*, which is non-conscious and as such actually undergoes transformation in the shape of the world. Invariably do we represent this world of experience as non-conscious (*jaḍa*); and it is the insentience of *Māyā* that gives the stamp of non-consciousness to the universe. The conditions of material causality (*upādānatā*), viz., that it must be the cause and at the same time be the substratum of the product[1] — is satisfied by *Brahman* also. The world as a product appears in and upon *Brahman*, and so *Brahman* is the material or the substantive

[1] The material cause is not the mere cause of the product; as this is common to the efficient cause also. It must be the substratum of the effect also. So, only a thing which produces an effect of which it is the basis, is the material or substantive cause. Cf. *kāryābhāratve sati kāryajanihetutvam upādānatvam* — SLS, *Ṭikā*, Benares edn., p. 72.

cause (*upādāna*). *Brahman*, the substratum, hidden by the power of concealment belonging to *Māyā*, appears as the universe, i.e., *Brahman* is the apparent cause (*vivartopādāna*). *Māyā*, on the other hand, is itself the really changing cause of which the world is the product of transformation.

Why Twofold Upādāna Is Admitted? The Psychology of Perception

The main reasons to justify the acceptance of the view of twofold material cause are these.

In the Advaita system, only the Ultimate Consciousness (*Śuddhacaitanya*) is regarded as self-luminous (*svaprakāśa*) and the Ultimate Reality is regarded as one and one only (*ekam eva*), and is thus opposed to all dualistic conceptions of Realistic systems of thought. But all determinate knowledge is essentially dualistic in character, and presupposes the existence and relation of two factors, viz., Consciousness and the material object. Leaving apart the question of the extra-subjective existence of the objective data, even the problem of perceptual knowledge presents a difficulty, viz., how can two independent entities, existing apart from each other, be brought together at all. The knowledge of a thing means that the object known and the fact of knowledge have been brought into a systematic whole. The existence of material objects is proved by virtue of such knowledge alone and not by any inherent prerogative of the objective datum. The material object being dead, inanimate, unthinking matter, cannot be supposed to illuminate itself and thus proves its existence, unless the light of knowledge be brought to bear upon it. For this, Vedāntic writers of the Advaita school have postulated a *tertium quid*, viz., the inner organ or mind (*antaḥkaraṇa*) which by its activity, technically called *vṛtti*, brings the two poles together and makes knowledge possible. The individual or subject consciousness cannot be supposed to move out, because all motion is predicable only of material objects. So it is the mind that moves out to reach the object. In the case of auditory perception, however, the object itself reaches the subject. It is immaterial whether the movement proceeds from the internal knower or the external object, but what is essential is that the relation must take place.

Now a question may be raised, — well, Consciousness being the only ultimate fact, how can there be any objective existence at all? The answer is — that the existence of the objective world cannot be denied as it is directly felt in experience, although the ultimate reality of such an existence is reargued both by logic and by Scared Revelation. So what we are concerned about in perception is to find an explanation of the situation and cannot remain satisfied with a denial of its existence. The fact remains that though unreal, the objective data somehow present themselves to Consciousness. The Monistic Vedānta holds that these objective data, though absolutely illusory, somehow exist on Pure Consciousness, and divide each into apparently water-tight compartments. So when even an empirical knowledge is supposed to take place, what happens is this: the apparent fictitious divisions are removed and the unity of Consciousness, underlying the different objective manifestations, is only revealed. So practically it can be said in the language of the poet that here — " The Spirit greets that Spirit". We have explained the philosophy of perception. It is, however, necessary that we should say something on the technical devices adopted in Vedānta on perception, which, however, have no other value than convenience of treatment and psychological explanation. The objective datum is not mere dead inanimate matter, but matter superimposed upon Consciousness. The pen is not mere pen, but Consciousness defined and determined by pen. Similarly the subject (*jñātṛ*) is not the mere mind, but Consciousness as determind by the mind. This is technically called the subject-consciousness (*pramātṛcaitanya*). The object is similarly called the object-consciousness (*prameyacaitanya*); and the modification of the mind (*vṛtti*) is called the instrumental consciousness (*pramāṇacaitanya* or *vṛtticaitanya*). These are purely technical devices, but are nevertheless necessary to explain all empirical knowledge in which the polarisation of Consciousness into a subject, object and cognitive process is a necessary condition. Unlike the Realistic systems of thought, the three poles are characterised as consciousness with the limiting objects qualifying it. The delimitations and divisions, however, are non-existent in pure transcendental Consciousness, but are felt owing to the working of *Māyā* or *avidyā*.

Let us now follow the process of perception (and particulary ocular perception) to a little more detail. As we have already stated, non-conscious material objects are not *directly* (i.e., by the right of an intrinsic prerogative) perceptible, since they are not self-luminous. Only when enlightened by something else which is self-luminous, these can be perceived by us. So we are to search for an illuminating source which is self-luminous. Advaitins called this the cognising subject (*jñātṛ*) — the *pramātṛcaitanya* (cognising consciousness determined by the internal organ). But this cognising subject, being situated within the body, cannot possibly illuminate the object directly, as it is situated outside. So an illuminating medium also is required. This is known as the *vṛtti* — the modification of the internal organ.[2] It has been called the illuminating medium, since it is non-conscious and as such non-luminous. Even the internal organ itself is not self-luminous, as it is also inanimate, and as such has no power to cognise other objects. But being the most proximate to the substratum consciousness (*svādhiṣṭhāna-caitanya*) and extremely transparent (unlike other non-intelligent objects),

---

[2] When the sense-organ (say the eye) is fixed on the external object, the internal organ undergoes a change and issues out through the organ (which serves the purpose of the door), goes to the object and takes its shape. This modification of the internal organ is known as *vṛtti* (particular mental state or mode).

it is the most fitted receptacle to receive the reflection of the consciousness on it. By its close relation with the consciousness which is reflected on it, it acquires the power of illuminating other less transparent objects. The opaque objects, too, though themselves unable to catch the reflection of the all-pervading Consciousness, can easily acquire the power (in a form, more or less illuminated) of reflection, when they come in contact with the transparent medium of reflection (*vṛtti*) — the modification of the transparent internal organ. Just as the walls, being opaque, cannot themselves reflect the face; but when splashed all over with water, they acquire some degree of transparency and serve as reflectors. Thus the internal organ serves merely as a mirror or a reflector, and its modification moves out of the body like an elongated ray of light or a stream of water, and takes the shape of the external object.

To take a more particular case, during the process of ocular perception, the eye is fixed on an external object. The internal organ, modified in the form of the *vṛtti,* shoots out like a ray of light (reflected by a mirror) and goes towards the object. Then the *vṛtti* assumes the shape of the object; and the object is said to be illuminated by the *vṛtti,* which is itself enlightened by the consciousness reflected on it. The non-conscious object is thus perceived by its indirect connection with the consciousness reflected on the *vṛtti,* but not by its connection with the *vṛtti* only; because, as we have already pointed out, the *vṛtti* itself being non-conscious, cannot possibly illuminate another non-conscious object; or, in other words, the veil of ignorance, covering up the form of the non-conscious object, being lifted up by its connection with the illuminating medium (*vṛtti*), the consciousness, particularised by the object, is reflected on it;[3]

---

[3] Up till now, it had remained unreflected on account of the opaque covering of ignorance over the object. *Vṛtti* gives the object transparency, and thus the object reflects the consciousness underlying it.

and the non-conscious object, while reflecting the consciousness, determined by it, gets itself illuminated. For, consciousness, being self-illuminous, illumines anything that comes in contact with it, provided that it has the fitness to receive and reflect the light of consciousness. So the expression — 'the object is perceived' — only means that the substratum consciousness, determined by the object, manifests itself by its unification with that determined by the modification of the internal organ. The identity between the consciousness particularised by the object and that belonging to the *pramāṇa*, or in other words, the appearance of the substratum consciousness as the external object is thus the defining feature of perception. As Dr Das Gupta puts it:

> Phenomenal creations are there in this world moving about as shadowy forms on an unchanging basis of one *cit* or reality, but this basis, this light of reality can only manifest these forms when the veil of nescience covering them is temporarily lifted by their coming in touch with a mental mould or mind-modification.[4]

It should be noted in this connection that Monistic Vedānta does not hold a brief for the theory of *vr̥tti* and this is evident from the fact that there have been authors who do not subscribe to this theory. After all, it is only a makeshift — a device — a mere hypothesis to explain the ultimate presupposition of all empirical knowledge, pre-eminently of perception, viz., the presupposition of the identity of the subject and the object, i.e., consciousness and the object. So Vedānta does not debar any other suitable hypothesis which can satisfactorily explain this fact of identification of the object and consciousness. It may not be out of place to mention here that this *vr̥tti* theory of perception is advocated in the Sāṁkhya philosophy also, and it is quite likely that Vedānta may have borrowed the theory from

---

[4] Das Gupta, *A Hist. of Ind. Phil.*, vol. I, pp. 448-51.

Sāṁkhya. The theory may appear to be crude and cumbrous, but has got to be adhered to so long as a better hypothesis does not present itself.

Now, to come to our point, we find that when with the help of the illuminating mental mould, the individual ignorance, concealing the particular object from our view, is temporarily dispersed and the identification of the object and consciousness takes place, — the particular unknown object is said to be perceived for the first time. What is true of the individual case, can also be regarded *a posteriori* to be universally true also by the process of correct generalisation based upon the careful observation of particular facts. Hence the Advaitins admit that when *Brahman* (i.e., Self-luminous Pure Consciousness) comes to be looked upon as identified with the objective world by the power of the cosmic *Māyā*, It appears as the world. Thus *Brahman* and *Māyā*, operating in unison, are said to be the joint material causes of the world.

The Phenomenality of the Objective World Implied in the Subject–Object Relation in Perception

The phenomenality of the objective universe can also be brought out if we examine the relation between consciousness and the presented data. The relation between the object and knowledge, we shall see, cannot be logically explained, but has got to be accepted as an ultimate fact. The relation of sense-organ (internal or external), too, cannot shed any light on this issue, because knowledge of God and the super-sensuous perceptions of the *yogins* are believed to come into play without the functioning of the senses. In the matter of the perception of external objects, the mind alone is absolutely impotent; so the super-normal perceptions, referred to above, cannot be explained through the agency of the mind. All attempts, therefore, of the Naiyāyikas to reduce this relation to simpler physical relations are proved to be futile. In view of this difficulty the later Naiyāyikas regard this relation as a unique relation subsisting between the subject and the object. It is called the subject–object relation (*viṣayatā*). But this formulation only assumes the very problem as a fact and does not make it any way simpler. The crux of the problem is — what precisely is the nature of the object itself? It cannot be something on which a special effect is produced by consciousness operating on it. What will be the nature of this effect? The Mīmāṁsists hold that it is something which makes the thing known by producing on it the effect called 'knownness' (*jñātatā*). This explanation is only a show and is a case of hopeless tautology. There is nothing to determine what will be known and what not. Besides, this hypothesis makes the actual existence of the object a necessary condition of knowledge. The result will be that no knowledge of past things or expectation of future possibilities will be possible.

Some, again, have sought to explain the object of knowledge as something which becomes the centre of practical behaviour consequent upon the knowledge of the object. But this seeks to shift the difficulty a step farther and leaves the problem as it is. There is nothing to determine the relation between the behaviour and the object concerned. Moreover, we are absolutely left in the dark about the meaning of 'behaviour' itself. For aught we know, it cannot be regarded as a physical behaviour, because no such behaviour is possible with regard to objects of knowledge which are non-physical in character, such as the self or thought, etc. Nor can the behaviour be regarded as something psychical; in other words, as the object of desire, volition and the like. The object of desire or volition is as much mysterious as the object of knowledge itself. So all attempts to reduce the knowledge relation to some other ultimate relations — psychical or physical — are doomed by their very nature to inevitable futility.

Let us examine the position of the Prābhākaras. Śālikanātha says that it is a simple thing — the object is what presents itself in a particular cognition. But the problem is — is there any ultimate determinant of what will be presented and what not? Leaving aside this ultimate problem, even the formulation on the face of it is vague. We do not know what we are to understand by this presentation *to* or *in* consciousness. Does it mean that the object is bodily taken into consciousness and integrated with it? This is absurd. Does it mean that it becomes an object of consciousness? If so, it is no explanation; that is the problem we are trying to understand. Nor does the subject–object relation become any more intelligible. There is no criterion by which we can regard consciousness as subject and anything other than consciousness as object, and why the relation should not be reversed. The situation does not become any more clear, if the object is regarded as a cause or condition of cognition. In that case the sense-organs, light and other possible conditions which make knowledge possible will have to be regarded as the object of knowledge — a plainly absurd issue. It may be urged, — well, not any and every condition of knowledge is the object, but only that condition which is perceived or cognised. But it is this fact of being cognised that is the problem which is sought to be explained. So such explanations are only statements of the problem itself and are designed, we are afraid, to evade the issue. But philosophers are desperate persons and there has been no end to their speculations, however absurd these may be. So there is a theory that holds that the object is that which becomes a determinant adjective of a cognition without any other relation, and the subject is that which is the substantial factor of knowledge. In the cognition of a table, the table is the adjectival factor and the cognition or the cogniser is the substantive, and no other relation beyond this exists. But this, too, is a *hoax.* Apart from the question as to what will determine the necessity of one thing being the adjective and another the substantive, and the question as to why the relation should not be quite otherwise, — the very formulation itself is defective. There may be cases of knowledge where the adjectival part is not believed to be the object. Take for instance, the judgement

— 'the knowledge of the table is inherent in me'. Here the fact of inherence is the adjective of the knowledge; but it is not perceived when the knowledge of the table takes place. It is, no doubt, comprehended in the subsequent judgement about the knowledge, but not in the primal perceptual cognition of the table itself, though the fact of inherence is a determinant adjective of the perceptual knowledge. If it is held that not any and every adjectival determinant can be the object of knowledge, but only that which is felt, it leaves the problem where it was. In other words, it does not explain anything.

The failure to explain the subject–object relation need not absolutely disappoint us. The foregoing survey of the historical theories makes the conclusion irresistible that all knowledge and the subject–object relation involved in it are facts which are not amenable to any logical explanation. It might, however, be urged that the theories under review might be failures, but this is no argument that no other successful theory will become possible. This is, however, a pious hope on the part of the Realist and is bound to end in disappointment. The failure of the theories is not due to any intellectual defect, but to the very nature of the object itself. And so all theories are bound to be failures. We can dispose of this issue by a very simple dilemma. Let the relation be anything; but it must be one which can be reduced either to a case of identity or one of non-identity and no third *term* is possible. Knowledge and the object cannot be held to be identical; because it will be tantamount to the denial of knowledge, which means the presence of two distinct and different things — one knower and another known. Nor can it be one of non-identity either; because not only the object in question but the whole world of things are non-identical with it. So there is nothing to determine what will be perceived and what not. If the two factors of knowledge, viz., awareness and object remain absolutely distinct and different, we do not know how there can arise a case of knowledge at all. But this knowledge arises and cannot be denied. So the Vedāntist declares it to be a manifestation of the infinitely resourceful *Māyā*, and not a real fact. Because reality cannot be self-contradictory, which the subject–object relation transpires to be.

The only difference between the Realist and the Idealist is ultimately a question of intellectual attitude. Experience (*pratīti*) is regarded by both the schools as an ultimate fact, with this difference that the Idealist insists that this experience must be a valid experience uncontradicted by logical canons or any other subsequent experience, whereas the Realist tries to avoid this issue when his fundamental position is jeopardised. The Idealist is a Rationalist out and out and is prepared to accept any situation that Reason may make inevitable, and in this no preconceived notion or theory stands in his way. The subject–object relation is a felt fact given in experience no doubt, but the Vedāntist refuses to accept it as true, because it is fraught with self-contradiction. The criterion of Reality, according to the Vedāntist, is that it must not contradict itself. And so only uncontradicted experience is the warrant of Truth and not any other.

The Nature of Avidyā and Its Relation to Consciousness

We think the account of epistemology of perception will remain incomplete unless something is said on the nature of *avidyā*. The *avidyā*, the Vedāntist is never tired of emphasising, is a positive entity. In other words, it is not a mere negation of knowledge. Negation of knowledge is a judgement and not a simple experience and as such presupposes the previous knowledge of terms. Now, negation of knowledge cannot be a negation of all knowledge, as it is itself a case of knowledge. So it must be something which is *not* negation. Its existence cannot be denied, as it is directly felt in experience — 'I do not know'. We reserve a detailed treatment of this important topic for the future, and it will suffice, we hope, only to indicate its broad characteristics. As we have said before, negation of knowledge is not an absolute negation, as it is also a case of knowledge in itself. Nor can it be a negation of specific knowledge, as no reference to specific objects is meant or given. It is a case of simple affirmation of ignorance — 'I do not know', — not that 'I do not know a particular thing'.

However may that be, a difficulty has been raised by Rāmānuja that this experience of ignorance cannot be reconciled with the fundamental position of the Advaitins that it is liable to destruction by knowledge, though its positive character may be taken for granted. Ignorance is not an eternal fixture, and the possibility of its destruction makes final emancipation a possible event. In that case it will have no *raison d'être* if its existence is antagonistic to Consciousness. The Advaitin here, Rāmānuja argues, is guilty of self-contradiction, when he says that ignorance is opposed to Consciousness, and still works in It. The Advaitin in reply points out that Rāmānuja here is labouring under a confusion of Consciousness (*sākṣicaitanya*) and knowledge (*vṛttijñāna*). Though in essence knowledge is also Consciousness, yet it materially differs from It in that it is produced by an accredited instrument of knowledge, — whereas Pure Consciousness is an eternal Existence. It is on the evidence of experience that we have to conclude that knowledge is opposed to and destructive of ignorance, and not unmodalised Consciousness. On the contrary, the latter is its very proof and foundation. We could have no knowledge of the existence of ignorance unless we were conscious of it. Sureśvara very poignantly remarks that this is a case of unpardonable petulance, when one contends that ignorance should not exist in Consciousness. Not only ignorance, but the whole empirical world is seen to be superimposed upon It.[5]

---

[5] *akṣamā bhavataḥ keyaṁ sādhakatvaprakalpane* ।
kiṁ na paśyasi saṁsāraṁ tatraivājñānakalpitakam ॥ — *BṛVār* I.4.1279

So we see that a difference must be made between Consciousness and knowledge, and it is the latter that is opposed to ignorance. To argue that the two should be regarded as identical in function, because of their essential identity, constitutes a case of inference, invalidated by approved knowledge (*kālātyayāpadiṣṭa hetu*) — just like the inference of coldness in fire.[6]

Now, after having indulged in this digression, which we thought to be absolutely necessary for a full comprehension of the problem, we may be permitted to revert to the old problem of causation as viewed by the author of the *Padārthatattvanirṇaya*.

The substratum consciousness by itself cannot remove the individual nescience, for it manifests ignorance also. But when reflected through the modification of the internal organ, the veil of ignorance is easily lifted. As we have already pointed out that there can exist no relation (such as contact or inherence) between the object (phenomenal creations) and the subject consciousness; for the subject and the object have one identical reality. The subject, however, possesses independent reality; and consequently the object is to be regarded as falsely superimposed on the subject.[7] In other words, the subject appears as the object, or the Ultimate Reality (i.e. Consciousness) is the apparent cause of the universe.

Māyā, on the other hand, is the really changing cause; since the insentient objects of the world are but the direct modifications of the non-intelligent formative cause — *Māyā*.

Thus according to the author of the *Padārthatattvanirṇaya* a twofold material cause of the world (*Brahman* — the apparent cause — *vivartopādāna* and *Māyā* — the formative cause — *pariṇāmopādāna*) is finally established.[8]

---

[6] *anuṣṇas tejo 'vayavī kr̥takatvāt ghaṭavat.*

[7] *Citsukhī*, N.S.S., pp. 44-47.

[8] *atrāhuḥ padārthatattvanirṇayakārāḥ — brahma* Māyā *cety ubhayam* →

The Vivaraṇa View: Īśvara (and not Brahman) — the Upādāna

The author of the *Vivaraṇa* opines that Personal God (*Īśvara*) and not the Absolute (*Brahman*) is the substantive cause.[9] This position of the *Vivaraṇa* is not fundamentally different from that of the *Padārthatattvanirṇaya* (given above), inasmuch as *Īśvara* is not represented to undergo any constitutional change in the process. If we analyse the entity — *Īśvara* (which is regarded as *Bimbacaitanya* (original Consciousness), and *not* the *pratibimba* (reflection), as the author of the *Saṁkṣepaśārīraka* thinks), we find Him to be Pure Consciousness associated with *Māyā*. Only the limiting adjunct *Māyā* changes into the form of the world, while Pure Consciousness undergoes no transformation whatsoever, but only appears to have changed into the world. While *padārthatattvanirṇayakāra* follows the analytical process, *vivaraṇakāra* adopts the synthetical one.

Dr Das Gupta's Interpretation of the Vivaraṇa View

Dr Das Gupta, however, is of the opinion that

> Prakāśātman Akhaṇḍānanda and Mādhava hold that *Brahman* in association with *Māyā*, i.e., the *Māyā*-reflected form of *Brahman* as *Īśvara* should be regarded as the cause of the world-appearance. The world-appearance is an evolution or *pariṇāma* of the *Māyā* as located in *Īśvara*, whereas *Īśvara* (God) is the *vivartta* causal matter.[10]

We are afraid that this position is not in consonance with the original position of the *Vivaraṇa*. In the *Vivaraṇa* the original Consciousness (*Bimbacaitanya*) as opposed to the reflected one (*pratibimbacaitanya*) is said to be the cause. And this ultimate

---

← *upādānam . . . . tatra brahma vivartamānatayā upādānam, avidyā pariṇāmamānatayā.* — *SLS*, Ben. edn., p. 72

9 *vivaraṇānusāriṇas tu . . . māyāśabalam īśvararūpam eva brahma upādānam.* — *SLS*, p. 59

10 Dasgupta, *A Hist. of Ind. Phil.*, vol. I, pp. 468-69.

Consciousness, as the original counterpart of reflection, is *Īśvara*, i.e., Consciousness as associated with *Māyā* as an adjunct. According to the *Saṁkṣepaśārīraka*, the original Consciousness is the Pure Absolute, and its reflection in the *Māyā* is held to be the Personal God or *Īśvara*. It is the Pure Absolute that is held to be the substantive cause and not *Īśvara*, who is rather a productive of *Māyā*.[11]

The position, therefore, comes to this: According to the *Vivaraṇa*:

(a) *Īśvara*, i.e., *Brahman* in association with *Māyā* (*Māyā-śabalam*) and not its reflection, is the *causa materialis*;[12]

(b) *Māyā* is always located in pure self-luminous Consciousness, and never in *Īśvara*, who is rather a concrete whole having Pure Consciousness and *Māyā* as His constituent factors; and[13]

(c) the entire entity *Īśvara* is not the apparent cause; the associated *Māyā* is the formative cause, while Consciousness alone appears as the world.

According to the *Saṁkṣepaśārīraka*, Pure Absolute, which is the final objective and goal of philosophical enquiry, is the original and is regarded as the cause of the world appearance. Of course, at first sight, this position seems to contradict the

---

11 *ajñānopahitaṁ bimbacaitanyam īśvaraḥ; antaḥkaraṇa-tatsaṁskārāvacchin nājñānapratibimbitaṁ caitanyaṁ jīva iti vivaraṇakāḥ.* — *Siddhāntabindu*, 109

ajñānapratibimbitaṁ caitanyam īśvaraḥ; buddhipratibimbitaṁ caitanyaṁ jīvaḥ; ajñānopahitaṁ bimbacaitanyaṁ śuddham iti saṁkṣepaśārīrakakārāḥ. — Ibid., 110

12 *māyāśabalam īśvararūpam eva brahma upādānam.* — *SLS* *māyopādhinirūpitabimbatvaviśiṣṭaṁ sarvajñatvādiguṇayuktaṁ ca yad īśvararūpaṁ brahmacaitanyam.* — *SLS Ṭīkā*, p. 50

13 *nāpi svāśrayacitprakāśena virudhyate 'jñānam.* — *Vivaraṇa*, Viz.S.S., p. 43

svayamprakāśasyāvidyāśrayatvam upapannam ity uktam. — Ibid., p. 46

position of the *Vivaraṇa*. But a compromise may be somehow effected, inasmuch as the causality attributed to *Īśvara* is capable of being extended to the Pure Consciousness forming His background, the associated *Māyā* serving only as an indicator (*upalakṣaṇa*).[14]

Saṁkṣepaśārīraka View: Pure Brahman — the Upādāna

The view of the *Saṁkṣepaśārīraka* thus deserves our attention next. In it *Brahman* Itself has been described as the substantive cause, and *Māyā* is regarded as a cause by courtesy only because it serves as the medium.[15] The service of *Māyā* is postulated, as Pure Consciousness in and by Itself is not susceptible of any change, which is made possible by *Māyā* serving as an auxiliary.

The Insentience of the World: How Does It Come In?

Here the question naturally arises, if *Brahman* alone is the material cause, wherefrom then does the insentience (*jaḍatā*) of the world come in? The effect derives its characteristics from the material cause alone and not from any other conditions. But the difficulty is only apparent, as it is not at all an unusual occurrence that the effect may derive some of its characteristics from even what is only a helping condition. This is seen to be the fact in the case of a pot produced from clay. The clay is made smooth and glossy by a particular process of kneading and these adventitious attributes are seen to be produced in the pot made of such seasoned clay, though the original attributes of the clay cannot be believed to be the cause. So the world may

---

14 *īśvaragatam api kāraṇatvaṁ tadanugatam akhaṇḍcaitanyaṁ śākhācandramasam iva taṭasthatayhopalakṣayituṁ śaknoti iti tasya jñeyabrahmalakṣaṇatvoktir iti.* — *SLS*, p. 63

15 *saṁkṣepaśārīrakakr̥tas tu brahmaiva upādānam, kūṭasthasya kāraṇatvānupapatteḥ; māyā dvārakāraṇam.* — Ibid., pp. 76

atra saṁkṣepaśārīrakānusāriṇaḥ kecid āhuḥ — śuddham evopādānam. — Ibid., p. 58

derive its character of insentience from *Māyā*, though it is merely a helping condition.[16]

Vācaspati's View

Vācaspati, the author of the *Bhāmatī*, also feels very strongly against calling *Māyā* the material cause of the world. According to him, *Brahman* is the apparent cause of the world. *Māyā*, on the other hand, is regarded as the instrumental cause (*sahakāri*) only, but never as the material cause proper.[17]

Vācaspati postulates two different types of *Māyā* or *Avidyā*.[18] The first is called the original or causal *Māyā* (*kāraṇarūpā*), and the second is the totality of the memory-impressions of previous illusions (*vāsanā*) possessed of the power of creating the appearance of the multifarious entities.[19] These individual *vāsanās* exist as potentialities in the causal *Avidyā*, and by an inherent energy are actualised in the perceived illusions. The causal *Māyā* is an identity existing from the beginningless time in the individual self. It has got a double function. In the first place, it functions as the repository of the *vāsanās;* and in the second place, it screens the Reality from our view.

Vācaspati Explains the Insentience of the World

The question of insentience of the world may be raised here

---

16 *akāraṇam api dvāraṁ kārye 'nugacchati* — *SLS*, p. 76. The commentator explains — *akāraṇam api* as *anupādānam api* — *SLS Ṭīkā*, p. 76.

17 *vācaspatimiśrās tu jīvāśritamāyāviṣayīkṛtaṁ brahma svata eva jāḍyāśrayaprapañcākāreṇa vivartamānatayopādānam iti Māyā sahakārimātram* — *SLS*, p. 77.

18 *Anirvācyāvidyādvaitayasacivasya prabhavato. . .* — *Bhāmatī*, introcuctory verse 1.

19 *svakāraṇe 'nirvācyām avidyāyāṁ līnāḥ sūkṣmeṇa śaktirūpeṇa karmavikṣepakāvidyāvāsanābhiḥ sahāvatiṣṭhanta eva* . . . — Ibid., under I.3.30, N.S. edn., p. 333; Also — *kāraṇabhūtayā layalakṣaṇayāvidyayā prāksargopacitena ca vikṣepasaṁskāreṇa* . . . — Ibid., under II.2.2, N.S.S., p. 494.

also. Vācaspati thinks that the insentience of the world is not derived from the material cause, but is an attribute natural with the effect. So there is absolutely no need to bring in *Māyā* as the material cause of the world to justify the insentience found in the product.[20]

Prof. Radhakrishnan, however, observes in this connection:

> The insentience (*jaḍatā*) of the world must be due to something else than *Brahman* pure and simple, and it is perhaps better to say that the world with its finite–infinite nature is to be traced to *Brahman-Māyā*.[21]

A Critical Examination of Vācaspati's Position

Prof. Radhakrishnan seems to think that Vācaspati has failed to explain the origination of the material world from Pure Absolute Consciousness (*Brahman*), and for this he believes that the service of a cosmic *Māyā*, existing in *Brahman*, must necessarily be requisitioned. We, on the other hand, are inclined to think that Vācaspati's explanation of the insentient world as an appearance over *Brahman* through the instrumentality of the twofold *Māyā* is neither inadequate, nor logically inconsistent. It may, however, be and has actually been attacked on other grounds which we are stating below.

Many an eminent writer of Vedānta has lent his support to this view of Vācaspati. Thus Acyutakr̥ṣṇānandatīrtha, in his commentary of the *Siddhāntaleśasaṁgraha*, while introducing the view of Vācaspati, explicitly states that the insentience of the world is not to be traced to its ultimate cause, but is a natural attribute of the product.

---

20 *jagaty anugataṁ jāḍyaṁ na kāraṇaguṇaḥ, kintu jagata eva svābhāvikam; atas tatsiddhaye māyayā upādānatvaṁ kāryānugatadvārakāraṇatvaṁ vā na kalpanīyam — SLS Ṭīka*, pp. 76-77.

21 *Ind. Phil.*, vol. II, pp. 552-53. In making this statement, Prof. Radhakrishnan seems to prefer the solution given by the author of *Padārthatattvanirṇaya* to that of Vācaspati.

This view of Vācaspati derives its final support from Bādarāyaṇa himself. Because, the objection raised by the Sāṁkhyas (in the *na-vilakṣaṇatva adhikaraṇa*) that the effect must be of the same nature as the *causa materialis* — sounds consistent from this point of view only. According to the *Bhāmatī*, the cause (i.e., *Brahman*) is intelligent but the effect (i.e., the world) is non-intelligent. The objection raised by the Sāṁkhyas can, therefore, be urged against this position of the *Bhāmatī* with the greatest force.

The answer given by the *Bhāmatī* is also very cogent; for the *Bhāmatī* states that every attribute of the product cannot possibly be traced to its material cause. In that case the difference between the cause and the effect would be indiscernible. The insentience of the world, for example, is not to be deduced from the material cause (*Brahman*), but is natural with the effect itself (the world). The *sūtrakāra*, too, supports this answer in the aphorism — 'But it is seen',[22] — where he declares that the objection of the Sāṁkhyas is without any force; since the homogeneity of the cause and the effect is not an essential condition of causality.[23] It is often seen that animate objects such as scorpions, etc., are produced from inanimate matter such as cowdung, etc. Thus a non-intelligent material cause (*Māyā*) need not be dragged in to explain the insentience of the world. On the other hand, those that assume a non-intelligent cause merely on the ground of explaining the insentience of the world, would not be able to make their position consistent with that of the *sūtrakāra*. The objections raised by the Sāṁkhyas and the refutation of the same by the *sūtrakāra* would be utterly meaningless from their viewpoint. For the reply given by the *sūtrakāra* to the Sāṁkhya

---

22 *dṛśyate tu* — *BrSū* II.1.6.

23 This principle is adopted on all hands by all sub-schools of the Advaita system and by Rāmānuja as well — in fact by all who have tried to refute the objection raised in this connection by the Sāṁkhyas.

objection distinctly points out that the homogeneity of the cause and the effect is not necessary at all. So it is the *Bhāmatī* only that has been able to grasp the true spirit of the *Brahma-Sūtras*, — while others, who insist on a non-intelligent cause (*Māyā*) to account for the insentience in the effect, would find it extremely difficult to reconcile their positions with the doctrine set forth by Bādarāyaṇa in connection with this topic.

It is for this reason that Vācaspati contends that the individual self (*jīva*) is the locus of *Māyā*. He finds no reason to associate *Māyā* with *Brahman* and to trace the causality to *Brahman-Māyā*, as almost other school of Vedāntic Monism and Qualified Monism have endeavoured.

Other Charges against Vācaspati

According to Vācaspati, ignorance rests on the individual self, because all our actual experiences of ignorance are of the form — 'I am ignorant' (*aham ajñaḥ*). On an analysis of the judgement it is found that it is consciousness as determined by the ego-sense that is the locative of ignorance. There can be no steadfast rule that the locus and the object of covering should be self-identical. Ignorance situated in *jīva*, therefore, can easily cover *Brahman* as its object, though the latter is distinct and different from the former (of course, from the empirical standpoint, where alone the question of covering by ignorance can rise at all). The authors of the *Vivaraṇa* and the *Saṁkṣepaśārīraka*, however, controvert this view saying that *Brahman* must be the locus and object of *Māyā*, since there is no incompatibility in the object and the substratum of a covering being identical and coincident. This is seen to be the fact in the case of external darkness. Darkness covers the very place in which it exists, and *avidyā* or ignorance is nothing but internal darkness and should have the same incidence. But Vācaspati contends that just as in ordinary illusions, the individual ignorance located in *jīva* covers up the consciousness particularised by the shell which is situated outside, so in the case of the original ultimate *Avidyā*, too, the object and the locus should be different.

The entire dispute turns on the interpretation of the common experience of ignorance expressed in the proposition — 'I am ignorant'. Vācaspati, we have pointed out, holds that the subject of ignorance is not unqualified Consciousness, but consciousness as determined and delimited by the ego-sense (*ahantāviśiṣṭaṁ caitanyam*). Ignorance is seen to be predicated of this limited consciousness or self. It will be wrong to hold, Vācaspati contends, that ignorance is predicated of Consciousness pure and simple. Because this interpretation runs counter to the unmistakable evidence of experience. Prakāśātman, however, does not accept the analysis of the illusory experience as offered by Vācaspati. He holds that the predicate in the judgement — 'I am ignorant' — is not ignorance only, but also the ego-sense. The two adjectives 'ignorance' and 'ego-sense' are simultaneously predicated of Pure Consciousness as the subject and the judgement follows as a matter of Course (*ekatra dvayam iti rītyā jāyamānaṁ viśiṣṭajñānam*). Mādhava, however, tries to reconcile the view of Vācaspati with that of the *Vivaraṇa*. He thinks that the difference between the two views is not fundamental. Though the individualised consciousness as *jīva* is regarded as the substratum of ignorance, still the real locus is Pure Consciousness which forms the background of the jīvahood. Acyutakr̥ṣṇānanda also lends support to this view. He says that Consciousness is the locus of ignorance and the individuality of the *jīva* only serves to determine the incidence of ignorance and certainly does not enter as a factor into the locus of ignorance.[24] So there is ultimately no difference between the two schools in the matter of Consciousness alone being the locus of ignorance. There is, however, a very material difference, viz., that Vācaspati does not subscribe to the existence of one cosmic ignorance or

---

[24] *cinmātrāśritam ajñānaṁ jīvapakṣapātitvāt jīvāśritam ucyate — Vivaraṇaprameyasaṁgraha.*

Māyā existing outside the individuated selves as an adjunct of the Absolute, — which is the position of the *Vivaraṇa*. The result is that Personal God becomes a matter of individual illusion and thus has no independent existence outside the individual minds. He becomes as much a product of individual ignorance as the phenomenal world — an apparent anomaly in which we have a man-made God instead of a God-made man, — the protests of *Kalpataru* notwithstanding.

Now, it has been urged against Vācaspati's conception of *avidyā* as residing only in the individual selves, the fallacy of logical 'see-saw' (*anyonyāśraya*) or mutual dependence. Vācaspati thinks *avidyā* is responsible for the defects of ignorance and as these cannot be conceived to exist in the Absolute, *avidyā* is incompatible with it. Its existence in the individual is, however, indisputable; so the individual self is regarded as its locus. But here also a difficulty arises. There is no denying the fact that *Brahman* is the only Reality and the existence of the multiform world and the multiplicity of *jīvas* or individuals is a false appearance due to the influence of *avidyā*. So *avidyā* must have a prior existence in order that the existence of *jīvas* may be possible. *Avidyā* is the cause of individuation and to make this *avidyā* dependent upon individuated selves is to put the cart before the horse. Individual selves are dependent upon *avidyā*; and to make this *avidyā* again, dependent upon the individuals for its very existence and functioning, is clearly a case of arguing in a vicious circle.

Followers of Vācaspati contend in reply that there is a case of reciprocal dependence in the very connotation of *jīva*. But this reciprocity does not involve any logical absurdity. Only those cases of reciprocity are vicious which make the independent origination or cognition of the things in reciprocal relation an impossibility. In other words, where a particular thing *A* can come into existence in dependence upon another thing *B*, and this *B*, again, is supposed to owe its existence to *A*, or the cognition of *A* is made possible by *B* and the cognition of *B* by that of *A*, — it gives rise to a logical fallacy. The implication is that this fallacy arises where the relation in question is one of causality. But in the present case, the relation of *avidyā* and the individual is not one of causality, but one of co-existence. And such co-existence of two factors, though mutually determined is not logically absurd, as it is attested in uncontradicted experience. To take a concrete example, there is such mutual dependence between a thing being a substance and being a subtratum of attributes. Now, the possession of attributes determines a thing to be a thing and vice versa. Or, as in a triangle, the attributes of triangularity and threesidedness are found to be co-existent and mutually determined without any question of priority or posterity. But this is not open to logical objection, as the relation, though one of mutual implication, is not one of causality. The existence of one is not brought about by the existence of another as a condition precedent. The two factors are co-existent as a matter of logical necessity. Had this relation been one between an antecedent and a consequent, it would have been a case of logical see-saw. The existence of the individual implies the existence of *avidyā*, and this implication is logical and not causal. The two factors are really aspects of the same thing, involved by an equal logical necessity in the very meaning of it. *Avidyā* and individuality are thus two co-existent facts logically involved in a self-identical situation, and no question of priority or posterity, therefore, arises.

Another objection is advanced against the position of Vācaspati regarding the causality of *Brahman*. Now, *Brahman* is regarded as the substantive cause of the world-appearance by all schools of Śāṅkara Vedānta, and this is held to be possible by the existence of a quasi-real principle, viz., *Māyā* in and upon *Brahman*. In fact, as we have made it clear, the world is but the effect of *Māyā*, and is regarded as the effect of *Brahman* because *Māyā* and *Brahman* are co-associated. According to Vācaspati,

Māyā or *avidyā* exists in *jīva*, and do the world as the effect of this *avidyā* should be regarded as the effect of *jīva*-cum-*māyā*.

But this will be in direct opposition to the accepted position of Vedānta. Vācaspati in reply contends that the location of *Māyā* is immaterial. It is the substratum of the world-appearance that should be regarded as the material cause. *Māyā*, though located in *jīva*, operates upon the substratum or *Brahman* and focuses the world-appearance upon it. Vācaspati thus succeeds in bringing his position into line with the accepted doctrine of the causality of *Brahman*; but that has been possible only by virtue of a forced interpretation of the concept of material causality (*upādānatā*). A material cause is defined as not only the substratum of the effect, but one that is possessed of productive efficiency. In Vācaspati's view, the productive efficiency cannot be predicated of *Brahman*. So one important factor is lacking. In this view, moreover, we are left with no means or criterion by which to distinguish between what should be a material cause proper and a mere locus. For example, the ground surface, on which a table rests, is a mere locus and not the cause. But in Vācaspati's interpretation, the locus should be regarded as the material cause which is absurd.[25]

And the fatal objection is that Vācaspati reduces Vedānta philosophy to pure Subjectivism, and Solipsism is but one step farther from it. The objective world may have an ontological foundation in *Brahman* which rather serves as the silver screen of the cinema show, but it has no extra-subjective status. For consistency's sake, Vācaspati cannot believe in the existence of the world when the individual ceases to perceive it, — "*Cessante causa cessat effectus*" — the cause having ceased to act, the effect ceases also. Belief in the existence of other thinking subjects does not improve matters. This would at most make the world inter-subjective, and so far as the objectivity of the

---

25 Compare and contrast the position of Vijñānabhikṣu who advocates the doctrine of locative causation (vide, Chap. 4).

world and its independent laws of existence and function are concerned, it is only a blank. The Idealism of Vācaspati is perilously near to the Subjective Idealism of the Vijñānavādins and of Berkeley and is thus exposed to all the consequences of their philosophy. It should, however, be noted in fairness to Vācaspati that his metaphysics is entirely different from the metaphysics of the Buddhists and of Berkeley in more than one fundamental respect. To be brief, Vācaspati is a Monist; the individual selves are a creation of eternal *avidyā* and they have no independent existence and are ultimately merged in the Absolute; whereas the Subjectivistic schools maintain the existence of a plurality of selves. Another momentous difference from the Buddhistic Idealism lies in the nature of the objective world. Though according to Vācaspati the world is but a manifestation of *avidyā* inherent in the individual, this manifestation is made possible only because the Absolute serves as its background. In the Buddhist account, the world is but an unfounded illusion. Vācaspati, therefore, insists that though a creation of the individual's ignorance, the world-appearance should be affiliated to the Absolute Consciousness as its cause, as it cannot emerge without such a substratum.[26] The individual and his ignorance rather serve as an occasion and as a condition only; but the world-appearance becomes possible only because it is supported on the Absolute. It would have been a purely subjective creation, if the world could come into existence without the assistance of the substratum. The causality of *Brahman*, therefore, stands unshaken, as without it the individual *avidyā* or *vāsanās* are absolutely impotent to bring the world into existence.[27]

Before bringing this review of Vācaspati's philosophy to

---

[26] Cf. *niradhiṣṭhānavibhrānter abhāvād ātmano 'stitā* ।
śūnyasyāpi sasākṣitvād anyathā noktir asya te ॥
— *Pañcadaśī* VI.76

[27] *Bhāmatī*, under Jagadvācitva adhikaraṇa — *BrSū* I.4.16-18.

a conclusion, we feel it imperative in view of the paramount position it occupies in the history of Vedānta that we should go deeper into the meaning of material causation. Of course, *Īśvara*, i.e., *Brahman*, endowed with a cosmic Energy in the shape of *Māyā*, is regarded as the material cause of the world in other school of Monistic Vedānta, pre-eminently the Vivaraṇa school. And this conception of *Brahman* as creating the world from Its own Self serving at the same time as its background makes the causality of *Brahman* more intelligible to our understanding than the conception of *Brahman* acting only as its substratum, as Vācaspati maintains. Though this interpretation holds good of a personalised *Brahman*, it is absolutely inapplicable with regard to the Impersonal Absolute. The *Vivaraṇa* cannot deny the causality of the Impersonal Absolute. But this causality can be possible only in the sense of Its merely being the substratum of the world-appearance. If it is maintained, as is really done by Appaya Dīkṣita in his *Siddhāntaleśasaṁgraha*, that Impersonal Absolute, divested of all relation with the cosmic Energy, is not yet an accomplished fact, but would emerge only after the exhaustion of the world-process with the emancipation of all the individual *jīva*s, — the view would be open to the charge of another extremism. Vācaspati may be ridiculed for making Personal God contingent upon the individual; but the other view makes the situation worse in making the Impersonal Absolute a future contingency. In other words, *Brahman*, according to this view, would be an imperfect, rather a less perfect, Being than the Impersonal Absolute, whom alone we can conceive as the most perfect existence. Had the Personal God been a perfect existence we would have no warrant to postulate the existence of another Ultimate Impersonal Absolute.

Kalpataru's Support to Vācaspati's Position

Amalānanda, the author of the *Kalpataru*, in his endeavour to save Vācaspati from the charge of Subjective Idealism, seeks to dispose of the theory of the conjunct causality of the *jīva*-cum-

Māyā;[28] and in doing so he evidently takes his stand on the theory of many souls (Anekajīvavāda) and not on the theory of one single soul (Ekajīvavāda).

In order to do full justice to the view mentioned above, we must first possess some acquaintance with the outline of the doctrine of one soul. According to this theory, the individual soul has three states of existence:

(a) The real *jīva* (*pāramārthika*) — which is Pure Consciousness, destitute of all adjuncts,

(b) the empirical *jīva* (*vyāvahārika*) — which is consciousness limited by the adjunct *avidyā* — only *one* in number, and

(c) the illusory *jīva* (*prātibhāsika*). These are mere semblances of individuals — reflections or limitations of the empirical *jīva*s in or by the internal organ. All the creatures of this world are, therefore, *prātibhāsika jīva*s.

The empirical *jīva* of this view can be equated with *Īśvara* of the *Vivaraṇa*. As according to the latter work, Personal God is the substantive cause, so here the empirical *jīva* (i.e., its substratum consciousness) appears to undergo the change, while the limiting adjunct *Māyā* is the real material cause.

So we see that if the theory of one soul is resorted to, the attempt made by the author of the *Kalpataru* to save Vācaspati from the charge of Subjectivism, becomes futile. Even if the theory of many souls is adhered to, the charge of

---

[28] *yaj jagatkartr̥tvam avagattaṁ tasya ca brahmaṇo 'nyatrāsambhavād ity arthaḥ.*

jagatkartr̥tvam anyatra Brahmaṇo neti ghuṣyati ।
vācaspatāv upālambham anālocyocire pare ॥

— *jīvāj jajñe jagat sarvaṁ sakāraṇam iti bruvan* ।
kṣipan samanvayaṁ jīve na leje vākpatiḥ katham ॥ *iti*

adhiṣṭhānaṁ hi brahma na jīvaḥ. adhiṣṭhāne ca samanvaya ity anavadyam.
— *Kalpataru*, N.S. edn., pp. 403-11

pure Subjectivism may somehow be subjected to the criticism put forward by the author of the *Kalpataru*. But ultimately the causality of *Brahman* is reduced only to a question of Its being the substratum or background of the world-appearance. And hence our criticism of Vācaspati stands unshaken, for all practical purposes.

The View of the Siddhāntamuktāvalī: Brahman — No Upādāna at All: Māyā — the Only Material Cause

The author of the *Siddhāntamuktāvalī* resents the very idea of attributing any kind of causal relation to *Brahman*, and affirms that *Māyā* alone is the material cause. *Brahman* is really no substantive cause at all. When *Brahman* is screened by *Māyā*, it becomes extremely difficult to differentiate the one from the other; and so *Brahman* is popularly recognised as the substantive cause.[29] The material causality attributed to *Brahman* is, therefore, only secondary, as It is the locus of *Māyā* which is the real material cause of the world. This view, however, is closely analogous to the position of Vācaspati, as both are agreed on the question of *Brahman* serving as the substratum of the world-appearance. There is, however, a difference with regard to the relation of *Māyā*, which is an adjunct of *Brahman* in the *Siddhāntamuktāvalī*, whereas *Brahman* is only the object according to Vācaspati. Another difference lies in the nature of *Māyā*, which is an adjunct of individuals in Vācaspati's view, whereas in the *Siddhāntamuktāvalī* it is an adjunct of *Brahman*, and so cosmic in character. But the most fundamental difference seems to be that *Brahman* is here regarded as the substratum of the world-appearance only through the medium of *Māyā*, whereas in Vācaspati's view It is directly the substratum, the *Māyā* having no *locus standi* in *Brahman*, being only an adjunct of the individual self. The Consequence becomes a

---

[29] *siddhāntamuktāvalīkr̥tas tu . . . māyāśaktir eva upādānam, na brahma . . . jagadupādānamāyādhiṣṭhānatvena upacārād upādānam.* — *SLS*, p. 78

serious differnce in outlook — *Brahman is* the real cause, being the immediate substratum according to Vācaspati. But the causality of *Brahman*, according to the *Siddhāntamuktāvalī* is only metaphorical and secondary, as it places the entire emphasis on the causality of *Māyā*.

The author of the *Muktāvalī* seems to take his stand on the *Vārttika* of Sureśvara,[30] whose view the author of the *Advaita-brahmasiddhi* puts very clearly in the following manner:

> It is true that *Brahman* is not the cause; but It has been called the cause by mere courtesy; becasue It is the substratum of *Māyā*, which is really the material cause of the world.[31]

These thinkers seem to feel that causality is a category that can be applied to relative order only and cannot be attributed to *Brahman* the Absolute.

---

30 *asya dvaitendrajālasya yad upādānakāraṇam* ।
ajñānaṁ, tad upāśritya brahma kāraṇam iṣyate ॥ — *BrVār* I.4.371

31 . . . *jagatkāraṇādhiṣṭhānatvena kāraṇatvopacārāt; tad uktam* —

brahmājñānāj jagajjanma brahmaṇo 'kāraṇatvataḥ ।
adhiṣṭhānatvamātreṇa kāraṇaṁ brahma gīyate ॥
— *Advaitabrahmasiddhi*, Bib. Ind., p. 177

4

The Doctrines of Emancipation Attendant on the Doctrine of Causation

The Question of Individual Release: The Attainment of the State of Īśvara — Appaya Dīkṣita's View

It would not be altogether irrelevant, we think, to refer to the interesting theory of Appaya Dīkṣita (which we have already hinted at while reviewing Vācaspati's position), which he has been at great pains to establish in the concluding pages of the *Siddhāntaleśasaṁgraha*. Appaya Dīkṣita maintains that *Īśvara* or qualified *Brahman* is virtually the only ultimate Reality existing up till now and the Transcendental Absolute (*Nirguṇa-Brahman*) is yet an abstraction. So the problem of causality has absolutely no reference to this Transcendental Entity and can be explained only by refrence to this Personal God. The Impersonal Absolute, though not an object of pious hope is, however, to all intents and purposes, simply non-existent. Appaya Dīkṣita, however, holds out an assurance that the Transcendental Absolute will emerge after the exhaustion of the world-process with the redemption of all personal selves.[1] So long, however, a single soul is in bondage, the Rulership of the Personal God will continue. This theory is too closely analogous to the theory of Samuel Alexander,

---

[1] *pratibimbo jīvaḥ, bimbasthānīya īśvaraḥ, ubhayānusyūtaṁ śuddha-caitanyam iti pakṣe tu muktasya yāvat sarvamukti sarvajñatvasarvakar-tr̥tvasarveśvaratvasatyakāmatvādiguṇapārameśvarabhāvāpattir iṣyate* —*SLS*, pp. 514-15.

the famous English philosopher, who in his *Space, Time and Deity* maintains the thesis that God is not yet in being, but will emerge after the perfection of the world-process. Alexander, however, does not believe in the present Rulership of Personal God like Appaya Dīkṣita. However may that be, Appaya Dīkṣita maintains consistently with his theory that the emancipated individual soul finds its unity with the Personal God and not with the Impersonal Absolute, which is yet a potential existence. We shall not go into a detailed examination of the aphorisms and other texts on which he bases his precious theory. It may only suffice to say that those aphorisms and texts are capable of an altogether different interpretation with equal if not greater consistency, as has been actually done by Acyutakr̥ṣṇānanda, the commentator of Appaya Dīkṣita himself. It should be noted in this connection that Appaya Dīkṣita seems to follow the position of the *Vivaraṇa* in believing that Personal God is only the prototypal Consciousness (*Bimbacaitanya*) and that there exists an infinite plurality of souls. We have, however, very honest doubts whether the position adopted by Appaya Dīkṣita can be really fathered upon the author of the *Vivaraṇa*. It is hard for us to resist the imperssion that Appaya Dīkṣita in this matter has been very profoundly influenced by the Śaivādvaita philosophy of which also he was a celebrated exponent.[2]

Apart from the merits of his logical interpretation of the texts, this curious theory of Appaya Dīkṣita leads to certain logical difficulties. In the first place, it involves an invidious distinction in the nature of Salvation attained by the different individuals in course of time. The Emancipation of the last individual will consist in establishing complete identity with the Transcendental Absolute, and salvation of his predecessors will be only an enjoyment of the sovereign rights and prerogatives

[2] Our conjecture is confirmed by a reference to the *Śivādvaitanirṇaya*, sections 3.2351 to 3.2355 — quoted in *The Bhāmatī Catussūtrī* (T.P.H. Oriental Series) — Introduction, p. xlvi.

of the Personal God, identified as they will be with the Personal Deity in the state of liberation. Another objection follows as a corollary from this position. The individuals will be emancipated in succession and not all at once, and so the period of their Īśvarahood will vary in length of time. The earliest of them will have to pass the greatest length of time in Īśvarahood and the penultimate individual will have the shortest enjoyment of this exalted position. Again, if the position that the emancipated soul becomes identified with Personal Godhead is accepted, it will be open to damaging objections. It is the special prerogative of *Īśvara* that He can assume any number of incarnated forms to satisfy the demands of his worshippers. The emancipated soul having no independent status apart from that of *Īśvara,* will then be subject to this contingency which is, however, expressly prohibited in the Upaniṣads. The emancipated soul has no association with a body, and as such is free from both pleasure and pain. It may, however, be maintained that such incarnations are only illusory creations and as such do not become a source of worry. Even if it is so amended it will go against the verdict of logic and scriptural texts alike. The Upaniṣad denies the subject–object relation in the state of Pure Consciousness attained by an emancipated soul.[3]

The entire issue can be clinched by the following dilemma. Does the emancipated individual feel his continuity with his previous unblessed condition or not? The first alternative is impossible; because the emancipated individual has lost all touch with his previous existence along with the disappearance of his individualising *upādhis*. The individualisation was the result of those limitations (*upādhis*) and the historic continuity of personal identity is possible so long as the conditions responsible for personalisation persist. The emancipated self has lost all relation with his past history along with the loss of his personality. The second alternative that the emancipated

---

3 *yatra tvasya sarvam ātmaivābhūt tat kena kaṁ paśyet . . .* — *BrUp* IV.5.16.

self does not recognise his identity with his previous condition of bondage virtually amounts to an admission of failure. This would mean that the emancipated soul will remain ignorant of his past history and so will not share the Omniscience of Godhood. In other words, the emancipated soul will be identified with God only so far as His essential nature as Pure Unqualified Consciousness is concerned. In that case, the emancipated condition will be in no way different from the individual's identity with Pure Consciousness, which is the position of those who maintain that in emancipation the individual becomes one with the Transcendental Absolute, which is above the condition of Īśvarahood.

About the contention of Appaya Dīkṣita that his theory of Emancipation represents the position of Śaṅkara himself, it will be sufficient, we hope, only to note that Śaṅkara emphatically denies all distinctions and gradations in the state of Final Salvation, attained by the saving Knowledge of the identity of *Brahman* and the individual. Gradations there are only in those relative forms of salvation which are open to the worshippers of Personal Godhood (*Saguṇa-Brahmopāsanā*). But such distinctions are absolutely absurd with regard to the individual who has received the Supreme Illumination. The contentions of Appaya Dīkṣita, therefore, lack consistency and logic alike. It may tickle the philosophic imagination as an ingenious curiosity, but it cannot give the metaphysical satisfaction which all our aspirations demand. Perhaps the Śaiva influence is responsible for this aberration on the part of so profound a philosopher as Appaya Dīkṣita was.

The postulation of Īśvarahood is only a question of religious necessity. We are going to take this point for a fuller discussion.

Bādarāyaṇa's Views about the Nature of Final Release

Let us examine Bādarāyaṇa's views about the nature of Final

Emancipation. He quotes two opinions of Jaimini[4] and of Auḍulomi,[5] the former holding that the *jīva* becomes invested with the highest attributes belonging to *Īśvara*, and the latter, on the contrary, maintaining that it is a state of Pure Consciousness unqualified by any attributes which are purely fictitious. Each of the two masters (*ācāryas*), however, regards the views of the other to be absolutely incompatible with his own. If the *jīva* takes the form of *Brahman* (endowed with the exalted qualities), it cannot be Pure Consciousness at the same time; and if it becomes Pure Consciousness, it cannot possess any qualities. Bādarāyaṇa[6] comes forward with the olive branch in his hand and effects an easy compromise between the two extreme views of Jaimini and Auḍulomi. He regards that the exalted qualities are not purely fictitious, but are superimposed on the Absolute by the individuated selves as a matter of religious necessity. Auḍulomi declines to accept this position, since according to him Pure Consciousness can never be the substratum of ignorance, — the two (Consciousness and ignorance) being by their very nature opposed to each other. Now, to come to the point, we may very naturally ask how Bādarāyaṇa reconciles these two conflicting views. Bādarāyaṇa assures us that Pure Consciousness can be accepted as the substratum of ignorance, inasmuch as it is the consciousness as reflected in *vṛtti* only that

---

4 *brāhmeṇa jaiminir upanyāsādibhyaḥ*" — *BrSū* IV.4.5, which may be translated as:

"By (a nature) like that of *Brahman* (the soul manifests itself); (thus) Jaimini (opines); on account of reference and the rest."

5 *cititanmātreṇa tadātmakatvād ity auḍulomiḥ* — *BrSū* IV.4.6. "By the sole nature of intelligence (the soul manifests itself), as that is its Self; thus Auḍulomi (opines)."

6 *evam apy upanyāsāt pūrvabhāvād avirodhaṁ bādarāyaṇaḥ* — *BrSū* IV.4.7

"Thus also, on account of the existence of the former (qualities), (admitted) owing to reference and so on, there is absence of contradiction (as) Bādarāyaṇa (thinks)."

is opposed to ignorance, but not so the Pure Consciousness, as we have already shown.

Difference between Appaya Dīkṣita and Rāmānuja Regarding the Question of Individual Release

Thus we find that both Appaya Dīkṣita and Rāmānuja hold that the attainment of the state of *Īśvara* is the state of individual release. While the former is of opinion that all the exalted qualities (including even the power to create and dissolve the universe) accrue to him in this state, since the individual soul then attains the state of *Brahman* endowed with all the exalted qualities (vide the view of Jaimini), — the latter differs from him in stating that the released soul exists inseparably connected with *Īśvara* (as a part of His Body) and possesses all His qualities excepting the special prerogative of creating and destroying the universe. Thus while Rāmānuja takes the aphorism —

"With the exception of world-business (the released possess all lordly power), (the Lord) being the topic (where world-business is referred to), and the souls not being near (to such business)",[7] — to refer to the state of Ultimate; Release, — Appaya Dīkṣita, in conformity with Śaṅkara's position, insists that the limitations spoken of have reference to the state of relative liberation (i.e., attainment of Īśvarahood together with the internal organ) invariably attained by the worshippers of the qualified *Brahman*, as Śaṅkara himself has explicitly stated.[8] The question of Final Release, according to Śaṅkara, is discussed in the aphorisms — *BrSū* IV.4.1.7; and he further thinks that the topic of the prohibition of the world-business (*BrSū* IV.4.17) has no connection with it, since the latter topic deals with the

---

[7] *jagadvyāpāravarjaṁ prakaraṇād asannihitatvāc ca* — *BrSū* IV.4.17.

[8] *ye saguṇabrahmopadeśāt sahaiva manasā īśvarasāyujyam vrajanti, kiṁ teṣāṁ niravagraham aiśvaryaṁ bhavati, āhosvit sāvagraham iti saṁśayaḥ . . . evam prāpte paṭhati — jagadvyāpāravarjam iti . . . "* — Śaṅ Bh. under *BrSū* IV.4.17.

question of a lower order of release (*saguṇa-mukti*) only.

Which of These Two Views Retains the Spirit of Jaimini?

As regards the question, whether the released soul, according to Jaimini, will possess all the qualities of *Brahman* (attributed to It on account of Its association with *Māyā*), Appaya Dīkṣita thinks that there is no positive proof that Jaimini seeks to exclude a few special prerogatives (such as those of Creatorship, etc.,) from accruing to the released soul. That this is the opinion of Bādarāyaṇa admits of no doubt. Rāmānuja, however, seeks to father the doctrine of limitations in salvation upon Jaimini also. For this he takes the particular *sūtra* (VI.4.17) out of its context and reads it with the *sūtra* dealing with Jaimini's view. But this is an altogether unwarranted procedure, as it is obvious that the *sūtra* (IV.4.17) opens a different discourse, and he will be a bold man who will read in it a backward reference. If this had been the intention of Bādarāyaṇa himself, he could have easily read the *sūtra* in question in the context of Jaimini's view.[9]

---

[9] Here Thibaut questions in his *Introduction to the Translation of Śaṅkara's Commentary* (S.B.E., vol. XXXIV, p. xix) on the *Brahma-Sūtras* that if Bādarāyaṇa cites Jaimini and Auḍulomi as his authority on this topic. Why does Śaṅkara represent him as criticising their views elsewhere (i.e., in the *sūtras* — I.4.21, IV.3.12, etc.)? The reply of the Advaitins to the above query would be that even if a portion of one doctrine be supported in one context, other portions of the same doctrine may be repudiated by the same author elsewhere in a different context. There can be no binding rule that because Bādarāyaṇa has given a partial support to Jaimini's view in one of his *sūtras* (i.e., IV.4.5), he should have to stick to this support of Jaimini regarding other topics also. It is for this reason that we find Jaimini's view refuted in several of Bādarāyaṇa's *sūtras* (viz., III.2.40; III.4.2; III.4.18; etc.). To be precise, even in the present context, Bādarāyaṇa does not subscribe to the position of Jaimini or Auḍulomi, but holds that they contain only half truths.

To conclude, we find that the *sūtrakāra* is fully in favour with the Advaita position that *Brahman*, as the substratum of *Māyā*, is the substantive cause of the world; and that the identity of the individual self with the Impersonal Absolute is the state of Ultimate Release, though the Īśvarahood may be ascribed to it by the rest of the *jīvas* in bondage. But we should advert to the necessity of causation in this connection.

The postulation of Īśvarahood is only a question of religious necessity. It is rather in the nature of a concession to weaker souls who cannot receive the highest Spiritual Illumination. The theistic bias of Rāmānuja is responsible for the confusion of a religious issue with a purely philosophical one. Personal Godhead has its necessity no doubt, and its justification in what has been called by Kant "*Practical Reason*", though in "*Pure Reason*" it has no *raison d'être*. Śaṅkara's logical mind has never allowed him to confound these two issues, which the muddled logic of Theists has failed to keep apart.

Different Types and Stages of Emancipation in Śaṅkara's School of Vedānta

The conception of Emancipation can be broadly classified under two heads, — regard being had to the question of ways and means:

(a) In the first place, the relative forms of emancipation which are attained by means of devotion of Personal Godhead.

(b) Second, the form of Emancipation achieved by trans-empirical Knowledge.

The first kind is again capable of being subdivided into three different types of salvation, the variations arising from the nature of the object of worship:

(a) In the first place, there are worshippers of Hiraṇyagarbha, the Demiurge, occupying a lower status than the Supreme Creator *Īśvara*. The powers of this Demiurge are rather of a delegated nature, and in the hierarchy of created beings, he is regarded as the first-born and the most exalted person. Now those who successfully follow the path of his worship, as prescribed in the Upaniṣads, are translated into the abode of Hiraṇyagarbha by a graduated course of journey through a hierarchy of blessed worlds as detailed in the Upaniṣads. Now, the question arises whether these blessed souls who reach the highest heaven are liable to a reversion to the cycle of transmigration. The answer to this question is not found on the surface. There is of course a definite statement of Bādarāyaṇa, based on the next of the Upaniṣads that these blessed souls reach their final union with the Highest Absolute after the cessation of the paritcular cycle of creation along with Hiraṇyagarbha when his term of office expires.[10] But Ānandagiri explicitly states that this holds good in the case of those spirits who worship the Highest Personal God, technically called the Causal *Brahman* (*Kāraṇa Brahman*), *in and through* His manifestation as the Hiraṇyagarbha, technically known as the Effected Absolute (*Kārya Brahman*).

(b) Those who worship only Hiraṇyagarbha without any reference to his Causal Background in *Īśvara* are, however, liable to revert to the world-order after the cessation of the existing cycle of creation.[11] This state of blessed existence cannot be strictly speaking called 'salvation' in any sense. It is practically on a par with the periodic residence in lower heavens attained by the worshippers of the particular rulers of these minor regions. The reason for

---

10 *kāryātyaye tadadhyakṣeṇa sahātaḥ param abhidhānāt* — "On the passing away of the effected (world of *Brahman*) (the souls go) together with the ruler of that (world) to what is higher than that; on account of scriptural declaration." — *BrSū*, IV.3.10.

11 *imam iti viśeṣaṇāt anāvṛttir asmin kalpe. kalpāntare tvāvṛttir iti sūcyate.* — Ānandagiri, *ChUpBh*. — *Ṭīkā*, IV.15.5. A.S.S., pp. 236-37

this difference of fate lies in the fact that Ultimate Salvation can be achieved only through the Supreme Knowledge of the Identity of the self with the Absolute. Now, the worshipper of *Īśvara* under the form of Hiraṇyagarbha has reached a state of spiritual progress which makes the dawn of the saving Knowledge a matter of natural sequence, — while his less blessed companions revert to the world-order for their spiritual deficiency, and failure to realise the unity of Hiraṇyagarbha with *Īśvara*.

(c) There is another category of blessed souls who worship the Highest Personal God directly and without reference to His lower forms of manifestation. Now, these persons, according to Śaṅkara, find union (though not *oneness*) with *Īśvara*, and as a consequence equally share with Him in all His glories and blessedness, except the special prerogative of the world-business (i.e., creation and the like), which exclusively belongs to *Īśvara*.[12] Now, though it is the highest station in an individual's life, consistent with the manifestation of his individuality, it is not the supremest form of Salvation, which is possible only in the merger of the individual into the Absolute Impersonal God. This Supreme Salvation is open only to those who have received the highest Spiritual Light and realised their unqualified unity with the Absolute. But the worshippers of Personal Godhead have got this privilege that they will reach beatitude in Final Release as a matter of course.[13] They have not to pass through the different heavens (which serve as different stations on the way to the world of Hiraṇyagarbha) like the worshippers

---

12 *jagadvyāpāravarjaṁ prakaraṇād asannihitatvāc ca* — IV.4.17.

13 *samyagdarśanavidhvastatamasāṁ tu nityasiddhanirvāṇa-parāyaṇānāṁ siddhaivānāvṛttiḥ. tadāśrayeṇaiva hi saguṇa śaraṇānām apy anāvṛttisiddhir iti* — *ŚāṅBh* under the *sūtra* — *anāvṛttiḥ śabdād anāvṛttiḥ śabdāt* — *BrSū* IV.4.22.

of Hiraṇyagarbha, and also they are not limited within the jurisdiction of Hiraṇyagarbha, and are not in any way dependent upon the fate of Hiraṇyagarbha for their release. So the worshippers of *Īśvara* reach a level of existence much higher and much more perfect than those of Hiraṇyagarbha. But still it is a lower state of perfection in comparison with the Final Release which means absolute identity with Unqualified *Brahman* in whom *Māyā* the principle of limitation has no existence at all.

We have fully discussed the theory of Salvation propounded by Appaya Dīkṣita, and we have found that according to him the highest form of practical salvation is the attainment of unqualified identity with Personal Godhead. And the Supremest State of Salvation implied in the identity with Impersonal Absolute is not within the access of individuals so long as the world-order is not exhausted. This Final Release can be reached only with the Emancipation of the last individual self. We have already subjected this theory to a critical examination and found it to be riddled with inconsistencies. But the most damaging drawback of this theory is that it makes the attainment of the Highest Salvation a mere matter of chance over which neither *Īśvara* nor, for that matter, the individual self identified with Him, has any control. The last soul is the luckiest of all; because, he reaches the Highest Salvation instantaneously, and he owes his good fortune to mere accident.

This attainment of unqualified Īśvarahood, Appaya Dīkṣita thinks, is accessible only to those who have received the highest Spiritual Illumination. About the *saguṇa* worshippers of *Īśvara*, he is in thorough agreement with Śaṅkara that their salvation consists in the attainment of the glories and powers of God minus His Cosmic Activities.[14]

---

[14] *. . . tesāṁ parameśvareṇa bhogasāmye 'pi . . . sakala-jagatsṛṣṭisaṁhā rādisvātantryalakṣaṇaṁ na niravagraham aiśvaryam, muktānāṁ tu niḥsandhibandham īśvarabhāvaṁ prāptānāṁ tat sarvam iti ahato viśeṣasya* →

Thus it is evident that the aphorism — "and on account of the indications of equality of enjoyment only,"[15] — refer to a lower form of relative salvation only and not to the Supremest Form of Emancipation; because, the individual soul, in the state of Ultimate Release, does not retain its character as a knowing subject. The knowledge of self (*ahambuddhi*) disappears, since the limiting condition (i.e., the internal organ which is a product of the *avidyā* belonging to each individual self) is also destroyed.

But according to Rāmānuja and other sectarian commentators, these *sūtras* unmistakably point to the state of Final Emancipation; and they affirm that the individual soul, as a part of *Brahman*, retains its self-sense even in the released conditon.

The basis of this fundamental difference lies in the acceptance and non-acceptance of the reality of the individual selves. The Advaitins regard the individual souls as unreal, as the limiting condition (i.e., *antaḥkaraṇa* — the internal organ) is false, being but a product of individual nescience. The followers of Rāmānuja, on the other hand, posit the *jīvas* as real — retaining their self-consciousness.

The Doctrine of Causation in the Śruti

The *sūtrakāra*, while aphorising:

> (*Brahman* is that) from which the origin, etc. (i.e., the subsistence, and dissolution), of this (world proceed),[16] —

and:

> (*Brahman* is) the material cause also, on account of (this view) not being in conflict with the promissory statement and the illustrative instances,[17]

← *sadbhāvāt* — *SLS*, pp. 514-17.

15 *bhogamātrasāmyaliṅgāc ca* — *BrSū* IV.4.21.

16 *janmādyasya yataḥ* — Ibid.: I.1.2.

17 *prakṛtiś ca pratijñādṛṣṭāntānuparodhāt* — *BrSū* I.4.23.

lays much stress on the Upaniṣad passages:

> That from whence these beings are born, that by which, when born, they live, that into which they enter at their death, — try to know that. That is *Brahman*. . . . From Bliss these beings are born; by Bliss, when born, they live; into Bliss they enter at their death,[18]

and:

> As, my dear, by one clod of clay all that is made of clay is known, the modification (i.e., the effect — the thing made of clay) being a name merely, which has its origin in speech, while the truth is that it is clay merely,[19]

which clearly indicate the nature and characteristics of the Universal Cause — *Brahman*.

The first passage declares the cause to be the Almighty Being whose essential nature is eternal Bliss. Other passages also may be adduced which declare this cause to be One whose essential nature is eternal purity, intelligence and freedom. That *Brahman* is omniscient we have been made to infer from It being shown that It is the cause of the world. The Upaniṣads have declared It to be so (i.e., of the nature of Consciousness) for hundreds of times and to confirm this conclusion, the *sūtrakāra*, too, continues as follows:

> (The omniscience of *Brahman* follows) from Its being the source of Scripture.[20]

---

[18] *yato vā imāni bhūtāni jāyante, yena jātāni jīvanti . . . ānandaṁ brahmeti vyajānāt, ānandāddhyeva khalv imāni bhūtāni jāyante, ānandena jātāni jīvanti, ānandaṁ prayanty abhisaṁviśanti* — *TaiUp* III.1-6.

[19] *yathā somyaikena mṛtpiṇḍena sarvaṁ mṛṇmayaṁ vijñātaṁ syād vacārambhaṇaṁ vikāro nāmadheyaṁ mṛttiketyeva satyam . . . sa ādeśo bhavatīti* — *ChUp* VI.I.4-6. This passage calls clay, iron, etc., to be true. But this does not clash with the Advaita position of the doctrine of Illusory Causation. The reality of clay, iron, etc., by way of illustration, only implies the reality of the material cause and the falsity of the effects.

[20] *śāstrayonitvāt* — *BrSū* I.1.3.

The origin of a body of Scripture possessing the quality of omniscience cannot be sought elsewhere but in omniscience itself. It is generally seen that the person, from whom some special body of doctrine referring to a particular branch of knowledge only originates (e.g., Grammar from Pāṇini), possesses a more extensive knowledge than his work, comprehensive though it be. What idea, then, shall we have to form of the Supreme Omniscience and Omnipotence of the Great Being. Which in sport, as it were, easily as a man breathes, has produced the vast mass of the sacred texts, known as the Vedas, the mine of all knowledge.[21] Thus from the Upaniṣads, *Brahman*, the Universal Cause, is known to be the plenum of Joy-Existence-Consciousness (*Sac-cid-ānanda*).

The second passage (*Chāndogya Upaniṣad*) — "as clay they are true" — asserts the cause only to be true, while the phrase "having its origin in speech" declares the unreality of all effects. The plain meaning of the passage is that if the true nature of a lump of clay is known, there are known thereby all things made of clay, such as jars, dishes, pots, etc., all of which agree in having clay for their true nature. These modifications or effects are names only, exist through or originate from speech only, while in reality there exists no such thing as a modification. In so far as these are individual effects distinguished by names they are untrue. In so far as these are clay they are true. This parallel instance is given with reference to *Brahman*; applying the expression "having its origin in speech" to the case illustrated by the instance quoted, we understand that the entire body of effects has no real existence apart from *Brahman*, the Universal Cause, the only Ultimate Reality.[22] Hence from the Upaniṣads' *Brahman* is known to be the apparent or illusory cause of the world-appearance.

---

21 *ŚāṅBh* under *BrSū* I.1.3, N.S. edn., pp. 95-99.

22 *ŚāṅBh* under *BrSū* II.1.14, N.S. edn., pp. 454-57.

Let us now go back to an earlier period to see whether the Vedic Saṁhitās give us any light on the topic. This interesting topic is discussed in the celebrated 'Nāsadīya' hymn of the *R̥gveda* (X.129), also quoted in the *Taittirīya Brāhmaṇa* (II.8.9):

> We find in this hymn a representation of the most advanced theory of creation. First of all there was no existent or non-existent. The existent in its manifested aspect was not then. We cannot on that account call it the non-existent, for it is positive being from which the whole existence arrives. The first line brings out the inadequency of our categories. The absolute reality which is at the back of the whole world cannot be characterised by us as either existent or non-existent. We cannot express what it is except that it is. Such is the primal unconditioned groundwork of all being.[23]

In this hymn the origin of creation is sought after in the form of a riddle and its answer:

> Whence (i.e., from what efficient cause) (it) has been produced, whence (i.e., from what material cause) is this manifold creation?[24]

The answer is that there was '*Darkness*' in the beginning:

> In the beginning (of creation) Darkness was there (the whole world) was hidden by Darkness — indistinguishable (i.e., unmanifested as it was in the form of a germ).[25]

Darkness (*tamas*) is to be explained here as the internal darkness of ignorance (i.e., *Māyā* or *Avidyā*), endowed with the power of concealment. Thus the Nāsadīya hymn, while hinting at the solution of the riddle put forward by itself, only

---

23 Radhakrishnan, *Ind. Phil.*, vol. I, p. 101, 1st edn.

24 *kuta ājātā kuta iyaṁ visr̥ṣṭiḥ* — *R̥V* X.139. 6.

25 *tama āsīt tamasā gūḷham agre 'praketam* — Ibid.: X.129.3.

Cf. *Manusaṁhitā* —

asīd idaṁ tamobhūtam aprajñātaṁ alakṣaṇam ।

apratarkyam anirdeśyaṁ prasuptam iva sarvataḥ ॥ — I.5

justifies the position of Sureśvara's *Vārttika* and that of the *Siddhāntamuktāvalī*, which hold that the causality ascribed to *Brahman* is only secondary (*aupacārika*), while that of *Māyā* is primary. In the above Saṁhitā text we get the following passage:

> All that was on all sides (the entire created world) was covered with (the Darkness) which was unreal (i.e., neither existent nor non-existent — false); (from it) that (world) evolved through the power of thinking (about the creation) (on the part of the Supreme Being),[26]

which clearly states *Brahman* was the one Ultimate Reality covered by the darkness of ignorance which is unreal (*tuccha*), and from which the world-order evolved through the power of thinking (or desire) on the part of the intelligent Reality. Hence *Māyā* is primarily the material cause of the world and *Brahman* is secondarily so, as It is the substratum of *Māyā*.

But there is yet another passage in the same hymn, which seems to controvert the position stated above:

> The objective world (together with its material cause *Māyā*) is of a lower order, and the (Conscious) Guiding Principle (i.e., the Absolute) is of a higher order.[27]

This passage declares that both *Māyā* (*Svadhā*) and *Brahman* (*Prayati*) are the material causes of the world. Of the two, *Māyā* is to be regarded as the lower (i.e., secondary) cause; *Brahman* is the higher (i.e., primary) cause. Almost all the Advaita sub-schools[28] are not very particular about ascribing the primary

---

26 *tucchyenābhav apihitaṁ yad āsīt*
tapasas tan mahinājāyataikam — *Ṛ̥V* X.126.3.

The *TaitBr* reads — *tamasas tan mahinā* . . . — which means that *Brahman* was the only fundamental unity covered *Tamas* which was unreal (*tuccha*), and from it the world evolved.

27 *svadhā avastāt prayatiḥ parastāt* — *Ṛ̥V* X.129.5.

28 Excepting the Bhāmatī school which denies *Māyā* to be the real material cause, Vācaspati emphasizes the point of making *Brahman* →

causality to *Brahman*, as they are only eager to establish It as the plenum of Joy, Existence and Consciousness, which are Its essential features (*svarūpalakṣaṇa*).

In winding up this discussion, we think it necessary to observe that the question of primacy or subordination is only a matter of emphasis. The undeniable fact remains that even in the Vedic speculations the necessity of co-operation between two factors, viz., Spirit and Energy, is regarded as indispensable for all creation. It is noteworthy that the element of Energy which is characterised as Non-Being or Darkness (*tamas*) is expressly stated to be an unsubstantial adjunct (*tuccha*). We shall not perhaps be making a too bold assumption if we are inclined to hold that this characterisation of the non-spiritual factor in creation as an unsubstantial fiction is perhaps the precursor of the celebrated Doctrine of *Māyā* as developed in Śaṅkara's philosophy of Vedāntic Monism.

← itself the primary substantive cause, as he contends that Pure Consciousness can never be the object of knowledge and that the Absolute cannot be intuitively known by means of *śabda* only (*Advaitadiddhi*—*jaḍatvanirukti*). He asserts that the Śāstras teach us about the lower *Brahman*, associated with *Māyā* or *vṛtti*. So according to him, *Brahman* concealed by *Māyā*, is the material cause of the world, as also the cause of *jīva*'s bondage. When *Māyā* is dispersed by *vṛtti*, which takes the place of the former, *Brahman*, determined by *vṛtti* (*Brahmākārā vṛtti*), becomes the cause of release.

5

The Conception of the Causality of Brahman in the Sister Schools of Vedānta

Advaitins and Vijñānabhikṣu

The position of the Advaitins, as interpreted in the *Vārttika* of Sureśvara and in the *Siddhāntamuktāvalī*, appears to be analogous to the position of Vijñānabhikṣu, who also regards *Brahman* to be the substantive cause, as It is the locative of the product. This position of the Monists differs fundamentally, however, from that of Vijñānabhikṣu, inasmuch as Bhikṣu never questions the reality of the effect anywhere. But the author of the *Vārttika* or of the *Muktāvalī*, in calling *Brahman* the substantive cause (as It is the substratum of *Māyā*), only asserts the phenomenal character of the product. We should like to point out in this connection that if Bhikṣu would only admit the phenomenality of the world and the function of concealment belonging to *Prakṛti*, his view would become closely analogous to, if not identical with, the view of the Monists. This point we are going to take up for a detailed discussion later on.

Advaita and Viśiṣṭādvaita

This view of the Monists seems to approach very near the view of Rāmānuja also, with the exception that like Rāmānuja the Monists never regard *Brahman* as subject to transformation either by Itself or through Its association with *Māyā*, and they never deny *Māyā* its veiling power. Now the question is to be considered whether *Māyā* is to be admitted as co-eternal with God in the capacity of His body or is to be regarded as indefinable (*anirvacanīya*) or false (*mithyā*) possessing the function of concealment. Rāmānuja depends on the former view, while Śaṅkara adopts the latter. Rāmānuja thinks that *Māyā* cannot conceal *Brahman* which is self-luminous Pure Consciousness, while Śaṅkara is emphatic on this possibility. We had occasion to touch this question in connection with our discussion of the epistemology of perception.

Thus, unlike Rāmānuja, the majority of the Advaitins (excepting the authors of the *Vārttika* and the *Siddāntamuktāvalī*) holds that *Brahman* is primarily the apparent or illusory cause (*vivartopādāna*).

The position is this: In both the Advaita and the Viśiṣṭādvaita systems *Brahman* is regarded as the identity of the efficient and the material cause (*abhinnanimittopādāna*). But while Rāmānuja holds that *Brahman* is the substantive cause, because Its body (*Prakṛti*) is the primary material cause — Śaṅkara thinks that *Brahman* Itself is independently the illusory or apparent cause.

The Position of Bhāskara

Bhāskara, on the contrary, after establishing *Brahman* as the identity of the efficient and the material cause, affirms that *Brahman* is Itself the really changing material cause. *Prakṛti* denotes the energy (*śakti*) of *Brahman*. Bhāskara is of opinion[1] that *Brahman* in creation spreads out Its creative power (*māyā-śakti*), and this radiation of energy is looked upon as the transformation of *Brahman*, though Its integrity ever remains

---

1 Bhāskara declares himself to be a follower of Upavarṣa: *kaḥ punar atra śabdo 'bhipretaḥ? varṇātmako lokarasiddher upavarṣācāryāgamāc ca* — *BhāsBh*, Ben. edn., p. 62. *prathamapāde pratyakṣādiprāmāṇyanirūpaṇaṁ codanāprāmāṇyasiddhyarthaṁ yat tad udake viśīrṇaṁ syād, upavarṣā-cāryasya śāstrasampradāyapravartakasyānuvaicitryaṁ kṛtam evaṁ vijñānavaicitryam* — Ibid., p. 124.

unaffected. According to Bhāskara, *Brahman* is possessed of a twofold energy, viz., (i) the spiritual energy (*bhoktṛ-śakti*), which is transformed into individual souls as cognising subjects; and (ii) the material energy (*bhogya-śakti*), which is transformed into cognisable objects as Space and the like.[2]

Rāmānuja, on the other hand, holds that *Prakṛti* is independently transformed and *Brahman*, too (as an organic whole consisting of the souls and matter in inseparable association), is regarded to have undergone the change, as the changing *Prakṛti* is the body of the changeless *Brahman*. Since the body cannot be separated from the *spirit*, the two are regarded as one identity and so the change is predicated of the whole and as such of *Brahman*.

Kumārila, in his *Ślokavārttika*,[3] seems to repudiate the view of Upavarṣa about the transformation of Pure Eternal Consciousness into the impermanent material world, on the ground of its breach of the law of homogeneity between cause and effect. Bhāskara, however, takes his stand on the authority of the Śruti and holds *Brahman* to be both eternal and at the same time the changing material cause.[4] Kumārila's views, too, cannot be said to be final on the point; since he contradicts himself saying that change and permanence are not conflicting, if the underlying unity is not destroyed.[5] Though the Self undergoes

---

[2] *apracyutasvarūpasya śaktivikṣepalakṣaṇaḥ* ।
pariṇāmo yathā tantunābhasya paṭatantuvat ॥ — Ibid., p. 98

tadananyatvam ity atra cāsmābhir uktaṁ śaktivikṣepalakṣaṇaḥ pariṇāma iti; īśvarasya dve śaktī bhavato — bhogyaśaktir ekā bhoktṛśaktiś cāparā; bhogyaśakteś ca sākāśādirūpeṇā-cetanapariṇāmāpatter bhoktṛśaktiḥ sā cetanā jīvarūpeṇāvatiṣṭhate. — Ibid., p. 105

[3] *puruṣasya ca śuddhasya nāśuddhā vikṛtir bhavet* — *Ślokavārttika*, Benares edn., p. 662, Sambandhākṣepaparihāra, verse 82.

[4] *śrutes tu śabdamūlatvāt* — *BrSū* II.1.27, *Bhās.Bh*

[5] *nānityaśabdavācyatvam ātmano vinivāryate* ।
vikriyāmātravācitve na hy ucchedo 'sya tāvatā ॥

→

occasional changes partially, the central unity ever remains undisturbed; and hence there is no fear of its total extinction (*uccheda*).

In the same way, too, Bhāskara justifies his own position. On the authority of the Revealed Text and the aphorism[6] where *Brahman* is expressly stated as undergoing change (*pariṇāma*), he holds that *Brahman* is at once changing and eternal. And the examples of clay and the like, which are really changing substances, are in his favour. Dr Ghate observes:

> The illustrations of clay and its product are distintly in favour of the Pariṇāmavāda (and makes it difficult to deduce the Vivarttavāda).[7]

The reply of the Advaitins to the above also deserves our attention. The Monists contend that the term 'clay' in the illustration (cited in the *Chāndogya Upaniṣad* passage) stands for the *cause in general,* but *not* for the formative cause alone. The reason for such a contention is this: The Śruti text, in stating — 'the clay alone is real' — emphasises the reality of the material cause only; and this is possible only from the viewpoint of illusory causation, since in the doctrine of formative causation both the cause and the effect are regarded as equally real. Hence Śaṅkara bases his doctrine of apparent causation on the authoritative statements of the Śruti; and his doctrine alone is really in accordance with the central doctrine of the Upaniṣads, as Thibaut has very clearly shown.[8]

Bhāskara and Śaṅkara

The main difference between Bhāskara and Śaṅkara is this:

← *syātām atyantanāśe 'sya kṛtanāśā 'kṛtāgamau* ।
na tvavasthāntaraprāptau loke bālayuvādivat ॥
— *ŚlVār*, Ātmavāda, śls. 22-31, pp. 694-96

6 *ātmakṛte pariṇāmāt* — *BrSū* I.4.26.

7 Ghate, *The Vedānta*, p. 81.

8 S.B.E., vol. XXXIV, p. cxxvi.

Brahman Itself is the substantive cause[9] in both the systems. While Bhāskara regards It as the cause that really undergoes change, Śaṅkara posits It as a cause that does not really transform, but only appears to change.

The Position of Nimbārka

Nimbārka, who likewise advocates the theory of the transformation of *Brahman*, has practically adopted the same view as that of Bhāskara. The followers of the Nimbārka school admit that mere arguments can never convince anybody of this apparently self-contradictory conclusion that *Brahman* undergoes a real change and at the same time Its permanent character remains unimpaired. It is entirely on the Śruti texts and the aphorism of Bādarāyaṇa (already referred to above) that they base their conclusions.[10] The transformation of *Brahman* does not imply the change of Its nature, but merely the radiation of Its power.[11] Keśava Kāśmīrin, in his *Vedāntakaustubhaprabhā*, clearly distinguishes between two different kinds of transformation:

(a) Transformation consisting of a real change of nature (*svarūpapariṇāma*), and

---

[9] The term *upādāna* is common to both *pariṇāmopādāna* and *vivartopādāṇa*.

[10] *na tāvat tarkabalenāsmākaṁ brahmapariṇāmābhyupagamaḥ; api tu 'svayam ātmānam akuruta' 'ātmakr̥teḥ pariṇāmāt' ityādiśrutinyāyābhyāṁ iti* — Devācārya, *Siddhāntajāhnavī*, Ben. edn., p. 115.

[11] . . . *brahma svaśaktivikṣepeṇa jagadākāraṁ svātmānaṁ pariṇamayya avyākr̥ena svarūpeṇa śaktimatā kr̥timatā pariṇataṁ eva bhavati* — Nimbārka, *Vedāntapārijātasaurabha*, Brind. edn., p. 356.

. . . *sarvajñaḥ sarvaśaktir apracyutasvarūpaḥ paramātmā evātmakasvādhiṣṭhitanijaśaktiviṣepeṇa jagadākāraṁ svātmānaṁ pariṇamayati* — Śrīnivāsācārya, *Vedāntakaustubha*, same edn., p. 357.

. . . *vastutas tu śaktivikṣepasya pariṇāmaśabdena vivakṣitasya brahmasvarūpapariṇāmānabhyupagamān na nityaśrutivirodhagandho 'pi* — *Siddhāntajāhnavī*, p. 116.

pariṇāmaḥ śaktivikṣepa eva — Ibid., p. 117.

(b) transformation implying a change brought about by the radiation of energy (*śaktivikṣepalakṣaṇapariṇāma*). The first kind of transformation is accepted by the Sāṁkhyas as their conclusion, since they advocate the self-evolution of an independent *Prakṛti*, not controlled by *Brahman*. The second kind of transformation is admitted by the followers of the 'Aupaniṣada' (Vedānta) philosophy.[12] According to them, *Brahman* (i.e., Śrī Puruṣottama) transforms His own Self in the shape of this world by the radiation of His own natural power which is co-eternal with Him, and is ever present in him. But in course of the radiation of His energy, His real nature remains unimpaired (*apracyutasvarūpa, nirvikāra*). The Śruti text is the only authority on this point.[13]

This radiation of Divine Energy is elsewhere described as agitation (*kṣobha*) in the nature of the Supreme Being. Prof. Radhakrishnan has very clearly defined it:

> The Śakti of *Brahman* is the material cause of the world, and the changes of Śakti do not touch the integrity of *Brahman*.[14]

Devācārya has explained it further clearly — transformation is but the manifestation of its subtle natural powers and the products contained in them in their subtler forms; or in other words, we call *Brahman* the material cause in the sense that It enables Its natural powers or energies (*śaktis*, viz., *cit* and *acit* in their subtle forms) to be manifested in their gross forms.[15] *Brahman*, again, is the efficient cause, inasmuch as It is instrumental in bringing about the union of the conscious

---

[12] By the term 'Aupaniṣadas', evidently Keśava Kāśmīrin refers to his school, since this doctrine is not unanimously accepted by all schools of Vedānta.

[13] Keśava Kāśmīrin, *Vedāntakaustubhaprabhā*, Brind. edn., pp. 358-59.

[14] Radhakrishnan, *Ind. Phil.*, vol. II, p. 759.

[15] *tatropādānatvaṁ nāma parāparakṣetrajñādipadārtha-bhūtasvābhāvikīnāṁ sūkṣmāvasthāpanānāṁ śaktīnāṁ tattadgatasadrūpakāryāṇāṁ sthūlatayā prakāśakatvam* — *SiJā*, p. 121.

individual selves (possessing the attribute of contracted knowledge) with the fruits of their actions and the means of enjoying these fruits of actions (body, etc.). Thus the creation of the universe is nothing more than the manifestation in gross forms of what previously existed in subtle forms, and that is eventually a sort of transformation.[16] *Brahman*, therefore, is both the efficient and the material cause of the world.[17]

Bhāskara and Nimbārka

Both Bhāskara and Nimbārka agree on this fundamental point that *Brahman* is the identity of the efficient and the substantive cause; but they differ in some other important details:

(i) Like the Monists, Bhāskara holds that though the individual self is by nature (*svābhāvika*) extensive (*vyāpaka*) in size (since by nature it is non-different from *Brahman*), it has the atomic size due to its limitations (*upādhis*, i.e., body, etc.).[18] Nimbārka, on the other hand, follows Rāmānuja in assuming the reality of its atomic size only.[19]

---

16 *nimittatvaṁ ca svasvānādikarmasaṁskāravaśībhūtātyantasaṅkucitabhoga-smaraṇānarhajñānadharmāṇāṁ cetanānāṁ karmaphalabhogārhajñānaprakāśena tattatkarmaphala-tattadbhogasādhanaīḥ saha yojayitṛtvam* — Ibid., p. 121.

17 *prakṛtir upādānakāraṇaṁ cakārān nimittakāranaṁ ca paramātmaiva.* — *NimBh*, p. 214.

. . . *nimittatvam upādānatvaṁ ca brahmaṇa āmnānād brahmaivobhayarūpam* — Ibid., p. 355.

brahmaiva nimittam upādānaṁ ca — Ibid., p. 356; also, vide pp. 245-46 and 348-60.

tat siddhaṁ jagadabhinnanimittopādānatvaṁ brahmaṇo lakṣaṇam — *SiJā*, p. 117.

18 *tad idam aupādhikam aṇutvaṁ jīvasyāto draṣṭavyam . . . jyāyastvaṁ tu nijaṁ rūpam* — *BhāsBh*, pp. 135-37.

19 *jñānasvarūpaṁ ca harer adhīnaṁ śarīrasaṁyogaviyogayogyam* ।
aṇuṁ hi jīvaṁ pratidehabhinnaṁ jñātṛtvavantaṁ yad anantam āhuḥ ॥
— Quoted in *SiJā*, pp. 56-57

(ii) According to Bhāskara, the non-difference alone is natural, but the difference is due to the limiting adjuncts. In this respect, Bhāskara's view seems to be at first sight analogous to the view of the Advaitins. But while the Advaitins hold that the non-difference alone is real and the difference is false (because the limitations are false), — Bhāskara maintains that both the difference and the non-difference are equally real (because, according to him, the limiting adjuncts are not unreal). But though real, the limitations are not natural; and consequently the difference, due to limitations, is liable to dispersion at the time of salvation.[20] Nimbārka, on the contrary, asserts that both the difference and the non-difference are natural and equally real.[21]

(iii) Again, while Bhāskara considers the co-ordination of

---

[20] *jīvaparayoś ca svābhāviko 'bhedaḥ, aupādhikas tu bhedaḥ, sa tannivṛttau nivartate* — *BhāsBh*, p. 243.

upādhikṛtabhedas tu so 'bhedabhāvanayāpanīyate, agnisamparkeṇeva kankagatamalasya — Ibid., p. 221.

[21] . . . *varīyastvaṁ svābhāvikabhedābhedamatasyaiva lāghavāt* — *SiJā*, p. 41.

Also vide the commentary on —

atha kimprakārakaṁ tad brahma . . . aupādhikabhedāśrayaṁ vā, jagadatyantabhinnaṁ vā, tadatyantābhinnaṁ vā, cetanācetanaśarīrakatvena tadviśiṣṭaṁ vā, svābhāvikabhedābhedādhikaraṇaṁ vā — Ibid., pp. 29-30.

In these pages (29-43), Devācārya criticises the views of Śaṅkara (Māyāvādin), Bhāskara, Rāmānuja and Madhva. The difference is not incompatible with non-difference. *Brahman* is the controller and the world is the controlled. So they are different in their respective nature and attributes —

brahmaṇas cetanācetanayoś svarūpeṇa bhedaḥ, itaretarātyantavilakṣaṇatvāt evam eva tasya tayoś ca sarvātmatvasarvaniyantṛtvasarvavyāpakatvasvatantrasattvasarvādhāratvādiyogena brahātmakstvatsanniyāmyatvatadvyāpyatvatattantrasattvaparādheyatvādiyogena cābhedaḥ — *SiJā*, p. 44.

knowledge and action as the essential means of liberation, Nimbārka disagrees saying that the knowledge of *Brahman* alone can lead us to salvation.[22]

Nimbārka and Rāmānuja

Rāmānuja holds that the relation between *Brahman* and the world is the same as the relation between the soul and the body. Nimbārka differs and characterises the relation as that existing between the governor and the governed. In regarding the world as an attribute of *Brahman*, Rāmānuja accepts more the principle of identity than that of difference, though according to him this identity is not absolute but is qualified (*viśiṣṭa*). But Nimbārka claims an independent viewpoint. To him the identity and the difference are equally real. If there be no difference between the attributes (both conscious and non-conscious) and their possessor — as also among the attributes themselves, there is every possible chance of intermixture of the three. *Brahman*, the governing — guiding — principle, is, therefore, independently existent (*svatantrasattva*), while the world has no such independent existent (*tattantrasattva*). Herein lies the secret of simultaneous difference and non-difference.[23]

Vijñānabhikṣu's Position

Vijñānabhikṣu, the celebrated author of the *Vijñānāmṛtabhāṣya* of the *Brahma-Sūtras* and the *Sāṁkhyapravacanabhāṣya* of the *Sāṁkhya-Sūtras*, strikes out a wonderfully original path in commenting on the *Brahma-Sūtras*. He calls *Brahman* — the locative cause (*ādhāra-kāraṇa*); and in the capacity of a locus

---

[22] *brahmajñānasya ca niratiśayānantaphalakatvaniścayāt* — Ibid., p. 18. Also vide *BhāsBh*, p. 2.

[23] . . . *api ca cetanācetana brahmādvaitābhyupagame 'pi brahmaṇaś cetanācetanābhyāṁ bhedaḥ tayoś ca parasparabhedaḥ svābhāviko 'bhyupagantavyaḥ . . . anyathā svabhāvasāṅkaryaprasaktiḥ; evaṁ bhedam apy aṅgīkṛtya punar viśīṣṭīṅgīkārātmakagauravād varīyastvaṁ svābhāvikabhedābhedamatasyaiva lāghavāt* — *SiJā*, pp. 43-44.

Brahman is the substantive cause of the world. Accordingly he points out that practically there can exist no such system as would reasonably admit *Brahman* to be the efficient cause alone.

Brahman: The Locative Cause of the Universe

Bhikṣu observes that like the changing material cause even the locative cause also should be regarded as the cause of the effect. Now, what are the characteristics and functions of this locative cause? The answer is that the locus of the changing material is a locative cause, inasmuch as the changing material cause exists, before the process of differentiation commences, in an undifferentiated condition in the locus, and also because it is supported and grounded in it. The material cause can work only because it has its support in the locus. So *Brahman* being the locus of *Prakṛti* (Primordial Matter) is locative cause of the world-process, because it is the ground and support of *Prakṛti* all throughout, no matter whether It undergoes differentiation or exists in Its undifferentiated state.[24] Now, non-distinction or non-separation of *Prakṛti* from *Brahman* is a relation *sui generis*[25] like the relation which exists between a thing and its character of being a locus, etc. Such relations are practically speaking one-termed. To take a concrete case, 'a red rose' is a proposition in which the relation between the attribute and the substantive is one of inherence. But the rose as a thing-in-itself and in its character as a substantive is not a self-identical concept, though

---

[24] *kiṁ punar adhiṣṭhānakāraṇatvam? ucyate — tad evādhiṣṭhānakāraṇaṁ yatrāvibhaktaṁ yenopaṣṭabdhaṁ ca sad upādānakāraṇaṁ kāryākāreṇa pariṇamate, yathā sargādau jalāvibhaktāḥ pārthivasūkṣmāṁśās tanmātrākhyāḥ jalenaivopaṣṭambhāt pṛthivyākāreṇa pariṇamanta ity ato jalaṁ mahāpṛthivyā adhiṣṭānakāraṇam* — *VijBh*, Ben. edn., p. 32.

[25] *sambandhāntareṇa viśiṣṭapratītijananayogyatvam* — *Nyāyakoṣa*. *Svarūpasambandha* (or the relation *sui generis*) has been very properly defined as — the relation which must be held to exist in a case where determinate knowledge or judgement (*viśiṣṭajñāna*) could not be effected by any other relation (*samavāya* or *saṁyoga*).

the difference is lacking and still the concept of a relation arises, the relation is regarded as one of numerical identity. The rose in itself is not anything different from its being a substantive so far as the question of numerical identity is concerned. But still the difference is discernible and so the relation is posited. The relation of *Brahman* and *Prakṛti* ultimately will transpire to be of this nature. It is of the nature of extreme non-differentiation due to an absolutely inseparable association of the two, and is responsible for the perception of unity between two distinct things (say, for example, milk and water). So though the effect can be affiliated to the locus as its cause, still the locus cannot be regarded as the changing material cause of the same. The material cause, properly speaking, is that in which the effect inheres. In other words, the inherent cause is the transforming material, and the locative cause is looked upon as a cause only by virtue of the peculiar relation existing between the locus and the inherent material. The thing is this: When the non-differentiation of the product is due to the relation of inherence (*samavāya*) between the cause and the effect, we find a case of the formative cause (*pariṇāmopādāna*). A piece of cloth is perceived to be non-different from the mass of threads that make it up. Here the relation between the threads and the cloth is one of inherence. Hence the mass of threads is to be regarded as the changing material cause or formative cause of the piece of cloth. But when the non-differentiation is due to the mere non-separation of the real material cause from the apparent cause at hand, we get a case of the locative cause only. Thus according to Bhikṣu, water is said to be the cause of the earth in this sense. Properly speaking, we cannot logically call water the real material cause of the earth in the same sense as clay is said to be the material cause of the jar. The question arises — then how can it be called an *upādāna* at all? Bhikṣu's answer is rather curious. Fine particles of the super-subtle element (*tanmātra*) constituting the earth existed in an undivided form in water at the time of the creation of the earth. These fine particles of *pṛthivītanmātra* gradually transformed themselves into this gross element — earth. The relation that existed between these fine particles of subtle earth and water was not one of inherence, but one of non-separation merely. Hence we can easily justify the purport of the Upaniṣad passage — 'Out of water originated the earth.' Of course, water cannot be the immediate cause of the earth; since the Śruti states that the subtler elements are the causes of the grosser elements; and the argument that the heterogeneity of nature is detrimental to causal relation, adds a greater force to this Śruti passage. In this way it is assumed that the elements sky, etc., are the causes of the elements air, etc., in the capacity of being locatives only. Vijñānabhikṣu thinks that the Vaiśeṣikas are not justified in making a futile dispute with the Sāṁkhyas when unanimity between the two systems can be thus very easily achieved regarding the doctrine of cosmogony. He points out that such a kind of causality is forced upon the Vaiśeṣikas also; but it is a case of perversity on their part to regard this locative cause as the efficient cause only. He would, therefore, admit a fourth kind of cause which is quite distinct from the inherent (*samavāyī*), non-inherent (*asamavāyī*) and the efficient (*nimitta*) causes. It is the *ādhāra-kāraṇa* or the locative cause. Thus Bhikṣu rejects the views of the direct transformation or the appearance of *Brahman* as the world. He concludes that at the time of creation, *Prakṛti*, which was located in *Brahman* in an undivided form, transformed itself into this world; and thus *Brahman* comes to be regarded as the locative cause of the world.

Śaṅkara, Bhāskara and Bhikṣu

Bhikṣu's position is fundamentally different from that of Bhāskara who advocates the theory of the transformation of *Brahman*, — and also from that of Śaṅkara who regards *Brahman* to be the substantive cause inasmuch as It is the substratum of the world. While Śaṅkara holds that the world is phenomenal, Bhāskara and Bhikṣu would make it real.

But however much Bhikṣu may try to bridge over the gulf between the Sāṁkhyas and the Vaiśeṣikas, as mentioned above, he may only succeed in so far as the unity in words is concerned. The real difference in their respective positions ultimately remains the same.

An Original Line of Interpretation of the Brahmasūtras: An Attempt at Compromise between Vedānta and Sāṁkhya-Yoga

Let us now examine the view of Bhikṣu in some detail. His main aim is to represent the Sāṁkhya system as non-conflicting with the Vedānta. Here arises a formidable difficulty. For the *sūtrakāra* denounces in unmistakable terms the Sāṁkhya–Yoga system in the aphorisms:

> If it be objected that (from the doctrine expounded hitherto) there would result the fault of there being no room for (certain) Smr̥tis, we do not admit that objection, because (from the rejection of our doctrine) there would result the fault of want of room for other Smr̥tis,[26]

and:

> thereby the Yoga (Smr̥ti) is refuted,[27]

respectively.

Bhikṣu champions the cause of Sāṁkhya–Yoga in the following way:

> The Smr̥ti of Kapila (Sāṁkhya philosophy) is authoritative, since it must have its scope. The denial of a Personal God in the Kāpila Sāṁkhya system is nothing but a *prima facie* proposition, borrowed from the doctrine of the wicked atheistic Mīmāṁsakas as a temporary concession to their

---

[26] *smr̥tyanavakāśadoṣaprasaṅga iti cen nānyasmr̥tyanavakāśa-doṣaprasaṅgāt* — *BrSū* II.1.1.

[27] *etena yogaḥ pratyuktaḥ* — Ibid.: II.1.3.

> views. That this is not the ultimate position of the Sāṁkhyas will be quite evident from the fact that the view of these Mīmāṁsakas also has subsequently been refuted by the followers of Kapila.[28]

So the denial of a Personal God or *Īśvara* is not the final conclusion of the Sāṁkhya system. To be a little more precise, it is absolutely foreign to the Sāṁkhya system. But the Sāṁkhyas have chosen to temporarily adopt it in order to avoid for the time being an unnecessary fracas with the vicious, aggressive Mīmāṁsakas, who are the real atheists.[29] Even the Sāṁkhya aphorisms appearing to preach atheism glaringly and in unmistakable terms, do but quote the sophistic chain of arguments invented by the godless thinkers referred to above. It is really an extravagant claim (*prauḍhivāda*) — a chain of reasoning adopted for a temporary compromise with the atheists.[30]

In making this bold statement, Bhikṣu contends that the real Sāṁkhya theory has neither been represented nor repudiated in the *Brahma-Sūtras*. As he himself very clearly says:

> So this division of the Sāṁkhya system into theistic and atheistic schools has for its basis the final and concessionary views of the Sāṁkhyas; or let the atheistic school be regarded as unauthoritative.[31]

Even he does not hesitate to call in question the authority of

---

28 *nanv evaṁ kāpilasmr̥teḥ kim aprāmāṇyam eva . . . na sāvakāśatvāt, paścānnirākartavyakumīmāṁsakānām īśvarapratiṣedhasyābhyupagama-vādena kāpilasmr̥tyupapatteḥ* — *VijBh*, p. 268.

29 "He also regards atheism as an unnecessarily extravagant claim (*prauḍhivāda*) to show that the system does not stand in need of a theistic hypothesis." — Radhakrishnan, *Ind. Phil.*, vol. II, p. 319.

30 *īśvarapratiṣedhakutarkā api parakīyā eva, 'tuṣyatu durjana' iti nyāyena prauḍhyā Sāṁkhyair anūdyante* — *VijBh*, p. 266.

31 *etena paramārthavādābhyupagamavādābhyāṁ seśvaranirīśvara-vibhāgaprasiddhiḥ sāṅkhyānāṁ vyākhyātā, artha vā kāpilaikadeśasya aprāmāṇyam astu* — *VijBh*, p. 267.

the *Brahma-Sūtras* in those places where *Pradhāna* (Primordial Matter) is denied the ultimate reality.[32]

The same is his attitude towards the refutation of the Yoga system in the *Vedānta-Sūtras*; the self-evolution of *Prakṛti* and the denial of material causality to *Īśvara* and other allied hypotheses of the Yoga system, which go against the conclusions of the Vedānta system, are represented by Bhikṣu as *prima facie* views held in concession to the supposed antagonists.[33]

So according to Vijñānabhikṣu, *sūtrakāra* has only demolished some misrepresented for spurious Sāṁkhya–Yoga theories. But the real Sāṁkhya–Yoga system has been left untarnished.

Now may arise the question that if the pseudo-Sāṁkhya–Yoga views only are refuted in the *Brahma-Sūtras*, how are we to account for the objection raised by the Sāṁkhyas in the next topic (i.e., Na-vilakṣaṇatvādhikaraṇa) that *Brahman* cannot be the cause and the effect is essential. The answer given by Bhikṣu is necessarily the same. This objection is not raised by the real Sāṁkhya school; but it was originally raised by the *kumīmāṁsakas* and temporarily adopted by the Sāṁkhyas as a *prima facie* view.[34]

Thus we find that Vijñānabhikṣu makes desperate attempts to reconcile Sāṁkhya views with those of Vedānta. He has tried mainly to show that the Sāṁkhyas also admit *Brahman* to be the identity of the efficient and the substantive cause of the world. The hypothesis sounds paradoxical, inasmuch as it is contrary to all received and accepted opinions about the Sāṁkhya system, and is in direct conflict with the current Sāṁkhya view,

---

32 *brahmasūtre pradhānādinirākaraṇam apasiddhāntatvād upekṣaṇīyam* — Ibid., p. 268.

33 *atrāpy abhyupagamavādena yogāprāmāṇyaprasaṅgaḥ* — Ibid., p. 272.

34 *idānīṁ sāṁkhyayogayor abhyupagamavādasya mūlabhūtaṁ kumīmāṁsakānām īśvare tadupādānatāyāṁ ca bādhakaṁ vedānteṣu kutarkajātam apākaroti pādasamāptiṁ yāvat* — *VijBh*, p. 273.

according to which *Prakṛti* alone is the independent material cause of the world. The current system of Sāṁkhya philosophy does not even tolerate the existence of God, not to speak of calling Him the cause. But Bhikṣu has forcibly thrust in a God in the Sāṁkhya system and calls him the identity of the efficient and the substantive cause, since he is the locative of the world really born out of *Pradhāna*.

Now, we may raise the question that if *Brahman* be regarded as the identity of the efficient and the substantive cause on account of Its being in reality the locative cause only, what would be the necessity of raising the objection (in the Navilakṣaṇatvādhikaraṇa) that *Brahman* cannot be the cause as It is of a different nature from the effect? Bhikṣu's ready reply to this is that the *pūrvapakṣa* represented in this section is not at all consistent with the real Sāṁkhya view. Similarity of nature between the locative and the effect is not regarded as essential by any school whatsoever. Elsewhere Bhikṣu cleverly shifts his ground saying that the expression *prakṛti* (in the aphorism — *prakṛtiś ca . . .*) stands for the power of God, and *Brahman* Itself is not the material cause of the world. From this standpoint also the topic (*adhikaraṇa*) becomes inconsistent.[35] Vijñānabhikṣu seems to contradict himself while commenting on the aphorism:

> Either the consequence of the entire (*Brahman* undergoing change) has to be accepted, or else a violation of the texts declaring *Brahman* to be without parts.[36]
>
> Where he accepts the possibility of the tansformation of *Brahman*.[37]

---

[35] *sākṣād brahmaṇo jagatprakṛtitvam api nāsya sūtrasyārthaḥ: asmin pāde śakter eva prakṛtatvāt* — *VijBh*, p. 259. Also — *svabhāvākhyā prakṛtir antaraṅgaśaktiḥ* — Ibid., p. 258.

[36] *kṛtsnaprasaktir niravayavatvaśabdakopo vā* — *BrSū* II.1.26.

[37] *nanu brahma cet pariṇamate tadā tat kim aṁśabhedānavacchinnam utāṁśāvacchinnaṁ pariṇamate* — *VijBh*, p. 293. Also — *. . . yathā devā . . . pariṇamante tathaiva brahma ity arthaḥ* — Ibid., p. 292.

Bhikṣu's Interpretation of the Adhikaraṇas Which Serve as the Support of the Theory of Abhinnanimittopādāna

It is a well-known fact that all the schools that profess to represent *Brahman* as the identity of the efficient and the substantive cause, base their argument on the *adhikaraṇas* (*Tadananyatva* — II.1.14-20, Kṛtsnaprasakti — II.1.26-29). Our curiosity to examine how Bhikṣu explains these two topics would be, therefore, very natural.

First of all, let us take up the 'Tadananyatva' section. Bhikṣu holds that *jīva* retains its individuality as the enjoying self (*bhoktṛ*) even at the time of emancipation and universal dissolution, since the Śruti states that even at the time of the transmigration of soul after death, knowledge and *karman* follow him together.[38] This is altogether a new line of interpretation — a complete departure from the traditional line of interpretation of the section. This interpretation is as original as it is curious. From the above, it would be evident to all intelligent students of Indian philosophy, that the peculiar Sāṁkhya view, followed in Bhikṣu's commentary, is not at all supported by the *sūtrakāra* himself. Bhikṣu, on the other hand, contends that the so-called pseudo-Sāṁkhya–Yoga system, as represented in the *Brahma-Sūtras*, is not the original Sāṁkhya–Yoga view, as adumbrated by him elsewhere.

In the 'Kṛtsnaprasakti' section, as we have already pointed out above, Bhikṣu seems to admit some kind of transformation on the part of *Brahman*, contrary to his accepted views.

---

[38] *tasya bhoktuḥ sopakaraṇasya prakṛta brahmānanyatvaṁ kāraṇe brahmaṇi nadīnāṁ samudra iva avibhāgaḥ . . . na tu bhoktur atyantaṁ brahmātmatvaṁ paralayādāv abhāvo vā, kuta etad svagamyate? ārambhaṇaśabdādibhyaḥ; ārambhaṇaśrutis tāvat — 'taṁ vidyā karmaṇī samanvārabhete pūrvaprajñā ca iti.* — *VijBh*, p. 279.

Madhva's Position

Madhva regards *Brahman* as the efficient cause only, and so his position differs fundamentally from all those commentators who posit It as the identity of the efficient and the material cause. So it would be needless to add that he differs from Bhikṣu also. But he agrees with Bhikṣu only on one point, viz., that this section (Tadananyatvādhikaraṇa) does not discuss the passage of the *Chāndogya Upaniṣad*[39] — 'The thing being a name only which has its origin in speech. . . . ' But for that reason his interpretation does not agree in detail with that of Bhikṣu either. He explains that the expression *tadananyatvam* does not really mean the non-difference of the effect from the cause, but that *Brhaman* was without a second at the time of creation. He takes the phrase *ananya* in the sense of *asahāya* (i.e., without a second helping hand, without any other assistant). *Brahman* took the help of no foreign material in evolving this universe.[40]

> According to him the question is whether *Brahman* wants the help of *karaṇa*s or instruments like ordinary agents in this world. The reply is that *Īśvara* creates the world without the help of any other instrument (*ananyatvam*) as is seen from *R̥gveda* X.81.2, in which all instruments, etc., are denied. And if there had been any such instruments they might have been known or demonstrated in the Vedas, but as a matter of fact they are not.[41]

The authoritative Śruti passage on this point is:

> What was the station? What was the material? How was

---

[39] *vācārambhaṇam* . . . — *ChUp* VI.1.4.

[40] *svatantrabahusādhanā sr̥ṣṭir loko dr̥ṣṭā; naivaṁ brahmaṇaḥ; svarūpasāmarthyād eva tasya sr̥ṣṭiḥ* . . .

paratantro hy apekṣeta svatantraḥ kiṁ apekṣate ।
sādhanānāṁ sādhanatvaṁ yataḥ kiṁ tasya sādhanaiḥ ॥
— *Mādhva Bhāṣya* under *BrSū* II.1.14

[41] Ghate, *The Vedānta*, p. 81.

> (it done)? (i.e., *Īśvara* did not take the help of site, matter or implements in creating this universe).[42]

So Madhva differs from the rest of the commentators[43] (including Vijñānabhikṣu also) and sides with the Pāśupatas in holding *Brahman* to be the efficient cause only. Accordingly he invents a new method of interpretation of the aphorisms —*prakṛtiś ca* and *ātmakṛteḥ*. . . . In the entire quarter (*pāda*, i.e., fourth quarter of the first chapter), containing these two aphorisms, Madhva only finds an opportunity to demonstrate that all words like *avyakta, prakṛti, śūnya, abhāva,* etc., without exception, ultimately refer to Viṣṇu. In fact, these words have been carefully derived in such a way as to denote Lord Viṣṇu and Viṣṇu alone. Of course, to the impartial students of Indian philosophy, these derivations would appear as specimens of philological curiosity only.[44]

In the 'Kṛtsnaprasakati' section also, he explains the aphorisms to refer to the doctrine of transformation. The objection raised in the aphorism (II.1.26-27, according to Madhva) would be valid if *jīva* is regarded as the creator. So he explains the aphorisms in the following way:

> If *jīva* is the maker, either he should exert his whole power

---

42 *kiṁ svid āsīd adhiṣṭhānam ārambhaṇaṁ katamat svit kathāsīt* — ṚV X.81.2.

43 Even Baladeva, the commentator of the *Brahma-Sūtras* belonging to the Gauḍīya school, does not follow Madhva in interpreting this section. The Gauḍīya school is known as an offshoot of the Mādhva school. But about this particular point, even the branch seeks to differ from the original root. *Govindabhāṣya* gives the traditional explanation that the effect (world) is non-different from the substantive cause (*Brahman*).

44 *Śūnya* — *śaṁ ūnaṁ kurute asau śūnyaḥ* — He who makes the pleasure (of others) inferior (to his own). *Prakṛti* — *prakarṣeṇa karotīti prakṛtiḥ* — He who performs well. *Abhāva* — *naiva bhāvayituṁ yogaḥ ato 'bhāvaṁ vadanty enam* — He is not capable of being meditated upon, and hence is called *abhāva*.

> in every little thing; but this is not seen; or he should exert a part of his strength (which is more reasonable); but that again would contradict the statement of the Śruti that *jīva* is without parts. So *jīva* cannot be an independent creator. But *Īśvara* can be so. His Creatorship is unquestionable, being established in the Śruti.[45]

> Thus Madhva is unwilling to call *Brahman* the identity of the efficient and the material cause. Though he favours the doctrine of transformation, he regards *Prakṛti* as the formative cause. *Brahman* is merely the efficient cause; but It guides *Prakṛti* in all her transformations.[46]

The Position of the Gauḍīya School

The Gauḍīya school, which professes its allegiance to the Mādhva school, seeks to differ from the latter about the doctrine of causation. Baladeva, the Gauḍīya commentator, declines to accept *Brahman* as the efficient cause only, on the following grounds:

> The Śruti establishes the proposition — 'If the *one* is known, *all* are known.' This proposition can be regarded as true, if we interpret the expression *one* as the substantive cause, and the word *all* as the variety of effects produced therefrom; since the knowledge of the substantive cause alone involves a knowledge of the products also. But a knowledge of the products is not possible, if only the efficient cause is known. The jar remains as unknown as ever, even if the potter be intimately known. *Brahman*, therefore, has to be accepted as the substantive cause of this world also. In the aphorism — *prakṛtiś ca* . . . (I.4.23), the word *prakṛti* means the substantive

---

45 *Mādhva Bh*, under *BrSū* II.1.27-28.

46 *prakṛtāv anupraviśya tāṁ pariṇāmya tatpariṇāmaniyāmakatvena tatra sthitvā ātmano bahudhākaraṇāt* . . .

avikāro 'pi paramaḥ prakṛtiṁ tu vikāriṇīm ।
anupraviśya govindaḥ prakṛtiś cābhidhīyate ॥
— *Mādhva Bh*, under *BrSū* I.4.27

cause (*upādāna*); and by the expletive *ca* (and) it is regarded as the efficient cause also. So the Gauḍīya school also regards *Brahman* as the identity of the efficient and the substantive cause.[47]

Brahman: The Formative Cause — Gauḍīya View

Brahman is both the efficient and the substantive cause; and It is the changing cause also. According to the explicit statement of the Śruti, *Brahman* is endowed with *three* different kinds of Powers or Energies — the Energy as revealed by the Lord's own nature (*Viṣṇuśakti*), the energy manifested through the individual selves (*Kṣetrajñaśakti*) and the material energy as displayed in the working of *Avidyā* (*Māyāśakti*). *Viṣṇuśakti* is technically known as the most exalted form of Energy (*Parā Śakti*). *Kṣetrajñaśakti* is a rather lower form of energy (*aparā-śakti*). *Māyāśakti* is the principle of activity, and is technically called *karmaśakti*. The *Viṣṇu Purāṇa* elucidates the point further. Through the medium of His Primal Energy (*Parā Śakti*), the Lord becomes the efficient cause; and through the instrumentality of the two other forms of energy. He comes to be recognised as the formative cause also. Thus as the efficient cause, He is changeless, but as the formative cause He undergoes real transformation. To be a little more precise, this change really affects the energies, since there is the well-known dictum — 'any injunction or prohibition regarding the possessor of an attribute applies directly to the attribute, and indirectly to the possessor of the attribute'.

---

47 . . . *avicintyaśaktikāt svayaṁkartrādirūpād upādānarūpāc ca* — *GovBh* I.1.2.

brahmaiva jagataḥ prakṛtir upādānam . . .

. . . *upādānavijñānāt kāryavijñānaviṣayas tatraiva śrutaḥ; sa ca nimittamātratābhyupagama na sambhavet; na hi kulāle vijñāte ghaṭo vijñāyate; tadanuparodhād viśvasyopādānaṁ caśabdān nimittaṁ ca brahmaiveti* — Ibid., under I.4.23.

The prescription of change applied to the Lord (in the capacity of the possessor of the energies in question) does only affect the energies directly; or in other words, the Lord is said to undergo transformation in revealing his peculiar manifold power, i.e., in the act of radiating His threefold energies. This transformation is, therefore, something materially different from that which is ordinarily understood by the usual connotation of the term.[48]

We should, however, note one point in this connection. Baladeva, while rejecting the view of Madhva regarding the doctrine of causation, approaches very near the Nimbārka point of view, in postulating the transformation of *Brahman* as the radiation of its energies. Thus he seeks to avoid the charge that *Brahman*, in undergoing change, would become impermanent.

The Position of Vallabha

Vallabha, the celebrated commentator of the Śuddhādvaita school, also upholds that *Brahman* is to be regarded as the identity of the efficient and the substantive cause. In his opinion, Pure *Brahman* is the substantive cause which transforms Itself in the form of the universe, without the medium of a body (as Rāmānuja asserts) or energy (as Bhāskara, Nimbārka and Baladeva hold). He successfully meets the objection of the Sāṁkhyas — *Pradhāna* (and not *Brahman*) must be the material cause of the world, inasmuch as the product (world) is similar (i.e., insentient) to it in nature; whereas *Brahman* is only the efficient cause. He points out that the knowledge of the inherent material cause alone makes all product known also. It is stated in the Śruti that *Brahman*, being known, nothing else remains

---

[48] *parāsya śaktir vividhaiva . . . iti śrutes triśakti brahma . . . tasya nimittatvam upādānatvaṁ ca abhidhīyate; tatrādyaṁ parākhyaśaktimadrūpeṇa, dvitīyaṁ tu tadanyaśaktidvayadvāraiva . . . evaṁ ca nimittaṁ kūṭastham upādānaṁ tu pariṇāmīti sūkṣmaprakṛtikaṁ kartṛ sthūla prakṛtikaṁ karma ity ekasya tadubhayatvaṁ siddham* — *GovBh* under *BrSū* I.4.26.

unknown.[49] So *Brahman* must be the inherent material cause of the universe. Like a lump of gold, It undergoes transformation, leaving Its integrity untouched. It is changeless, and at the same time changing. This may appear to be contradictory to all logical arguments; but this is the peculiarity of the nature of *Brahman*. This peculiarity is absent in any other object of the universe. The only authority on this point is Śruti, as Vallabha shows in his commentary on the aphorism:

> But (this is not so), on account of scriptural passages, and on account of (*Brahman*) resting on Scripture (only).[50]

This view of Vallabha is known as the doctrine of the transformation of Pure *Brahman* (Śuddhabrahmapariṇāmavāda).

Two Main Divisions of the Commentators of the Brahma-Sūtras Accepting Brahman as the Identity of the Efficient and the Substantive Cause

Thus it is evident that excepting Madhva and the Pāśupata Śaivas, the rest of the principal commentators on the *Brahma-Sūtras* are unanimous in regarding *Brahman* as both the efficient and the substantive cause. But this identity of the efficient and the substantive cause, as interpreted by Vijñānabhikṣu, is something fundamentally different from that as admitted by Śaṅkara, Bhāskara, Rāmānuja, Śrīkaṇṭha,[51] Nimbārka

---

49 . . . *samavāyikāraṇajñāne hi kāryajñānam . . . tasmād brahmaiva samavāyikāraṇam, na prakṛtiḥ* — *ValBh*, under *BrSu* I.4.23.

tadāmānaṁ svayam akutruta iti svasyaiva karmakartṛbhāvāt; sukṛtavacanāc ca alaukikatvam . . . pariṇamate kāryākāreṇa iti; avikṛtam eva pariṇamate suvarṇam . . . vakṣyati ca 'śrutes tu śabdamūlatvāt' iti — Ibid., under *BrSu* I.4.26.

50 *śruteś tu śabdamūlatvāt* — *BrSū* II.1.27.

51 Śrīkaṇṭha does not follow Pāśupata Śaivism (which maintains that the Lord is the operative cause only), refuted in the *Brahma-Sūtras* (II.2.37-41). He closely follows Rāmānuja with simple adaptations wherever necessary, and has merely substitued Śiva in place of Rāmānuja's Viṣṇu.

and Vallabha. The latter are unanimous in their opinion that Bādarāyaṇa positively refutes the theory that God is merely the efficient cause of the world in the section (*adhikaraṇa*), beginning with the aphorism:

> The Lord (cannot be the operative cause of the world only) on account of the inappropriateness (of that doctrine).[52]

In this particular section the *sūtrakāra* applies himself to the refutation of the doctrine according to which the Lord is the cause of the world only in so far as He is the general Ruler. In the previous sections of the work, the *sūtrakāra* himself has proved that the Lord is the identity of the efficient and the substantive cause. Hence, if the present section were meant to impugn the doctrine of Lord's Rulership in general, the earlier and later parts of the work would be mutually contradictory, and Bādarāyaṇa would be guilty of the fault of self-contradiction. It should be assumed, therefore, that the purport of the section is to refute the doctrine of those who maintain that God is not the material cause, but merely the Ruler — the operative cause of the world.

Bhikṣu, on the other hand, comments on the above section in the following way:

> God should not be regarded as an object of mere inference.[53] His existence may be proved by inference based on Śruti only. This proposition has already been established in the aphorism —
>
> (The omniscience of *Brahman*) follows from Its being the source of Scripture.[54]

---

52 *Patyur asāmañjasyāt* and the following three *sūtras*, constituting the *adhikaraṇa*, II.2.37-41.

53 *na patyur īśvarasyānumānaṁ sambhavati* — *VijBh*, p. 318.

54 *śāstrayonitvāt* — *BrSū* I.1.3.

śāstraṁ yonir mūlapramāṇaṁ yasminn iti śāstrayoni . . . astra śāstrād iti vaktavye śāstrayonitvād ity uktaṁ śāstrāviruddhānumānādīnāṁ grahaṇāya — *VijBh*, p. 69.

Hence it is clear that the Śruti alone is the independent means of proof about the existence of God, and inference based on Śruti is also regarded as a secondary means of proof.

If, however, any doubt arises as to why this section was incorporated at all in the body of the work of Bādarāyaṇa, the answer is that it is included only to make the position clearer.

The Particular Sections of the Brahma-Sūtras Dealing with the Doctrine of Causation

It would be clear from the foregoing discussions that the five *adhikaraṇas*, viz.,

(a) Janmādyādhikaraṇa (*BrSū* I.1.2),

(b) Prakṛtyādhikaraṇa (Ibid., I.4.23-27),

(c) Na-vilakṣaṇatvādhikaraṇa (Ibid., II.1.4-11),

(d) Tadananyatvādhikaraṇa (Ibid., II.1.14-20), and

(e) Kṛtsnaprasaktyādhikaraṇa (Ibid., II.2.26-29),

are the mainstay of the doctrine that *Brahman* is the identity of the efficient and the substantive cause of the world (*jagadabhinnanimittopādāna*).

We are now in a position to enquire into the question as to which of the schools of Vedānta gives us the most faithful representation of the view of Bādarāyaṇa regarding the nature of causality attributed to *Brahman*. In doing so we shall be required to take into account the consistency of the *five* sections (*adhikaraṇas*) mentioned above, with regard to the different schools of Vedānta already referred to. And it may be observed without any attempt to anticipate the result of our findings that the interpretation of *Brahman*'s causality as offered by Śaṅkara gives the greatest satisfaction to the demands of logic, and this has been sufficiently made clear, we hope, in the section where Śaṅkara's interpretation of causality has been discussed by us. The unreality of causality is a conclusion which irresistibly follows from both the texts of the Upaniṣads and logical consistency.

Bibliography

Advaitabrahmasiddhi, Bibliographica Indica, Calcutta: Asiatic Society of Bengal, 1890.

Advaitasiddhi, Nirnayasagar Press edn, Bombay, 1937.

Dasgupta, Surendranath, 1922, *A History of Indian Philosophy*, vol. I, Cambridge: Cambridge University Press.

Devācārya, *Siddhāntajāhnavī*, Benares edn.

Ghate, V.S., 1926, *The Vedānta*, Pune: Oriental Book Agency.

Gosawmin, Jiva, *Satsandarbha*.

Kalpataru, Nirnayasagar edn., Bombay.

Keśava Kāśmīrin, *Vedāntakaustubhaprabhā*, Brind. edn.

Madhva, *Sarvadarśanasaṁgraha*, A.S.S. edn.

——— *Vijnanamrta Bhasya* on *Brahma-Sutras*.

Nimbārka, *Vedāntapārijātasaurabha*, Brind. edn.

Nyāyamañjarī, V.S.S. edn.

Radhakrishnan, S., 1923/27, *Indian Philosophy*, first edition, vols. I-II, Oxford: Oxford University Press.

Rhys Davids, T.W., 1980/84, *Milindapanha*, vols. I and II, Sacred Books of the East Series, vol. XXXIV, Oxford: Clarendon Press.

Sankara, *Anandamayadhikarana*.

Śaṅkara's *Bhāṣya* on the *Brahma-Sūtras*, Nirnayasagara edn.

Sastri, S. Kuppusvami, 1925, "The Bodhayana and Dramidacarya, Two Old vedantins Presupposed by Ramanuja", in *Proceedings and Transactions of the Third Oriental Conference*, pp. 465-68, Madras: The Law Printing House.

Śāstrī, A.K., 1930, *Vedāntaparibhāṣā*, second edn., Calcutta: University of Calcutta.

——— *Vedanta Parbhasha.*

Ślokavārttika, Benares edn., 1898-99, Benares: Chowkhamba Sanskrit Series.

Śrī Bhāṣya, S.S.S., Chowkhamba Sanskrit Series.

Śrīharṣa, *Khaṇḍanakhaṇḍakhādya*, Chowkhamba Sanskrit Series.

Śrīnivāsācārya, *Vedāntakaustubha*, Brind. edn.

Stcherbatsky, Th, 1927, *The Conception of Buddhist Nirvāṇa*, Leningrad: Institute of Buddhist Culture.

Tattvadīpana, A.K. Śāstrī's edn.

The Bhāmatī Catussūtrī, Theosophical Publishing House Series, Madras, 1933.

Thibaut, Georg, 1890, *Vedantasutra* with the commentary of Sankara, tr. with Introduction, Sacred Books of the East, vol. XXXIV, Oxford: Clarendon Press.

Vaiyākaraṇasiddhāntamañjūṣā of Nāgeśa Bhaṭṭa with the commentary *Kuñjikā* by Durbalācārya, Chowkhamba Sanskrit Series.

Vidyabhusana, Baladeva, *Govinda Bhasya on the Brahma-Sutras.*

Vidyāsāgarī, Chowkhamba Sanskrit Series.

Vivaraṇaprameyasaṁgraha, V.S.S., Benares, 1893.

Index

abhāva 99
abheda 17, 21
abhinnanimittopādāna 11-12, 82
  theory of 97
Absolute
  Being 5, 25
  Bliss 5, 28
  Consciousness 5, 15, 21, 28, 34, 59
  Existence 17, 28
  nature of 20
  Non-Being 25
  of Vedānta 29
  Self 6
ācāryas 68
Acintyabhedābhedavāda 1
acit 86
Acyutakṛṣṇānanda 55
Acyutakṛṣṇānandatīrtha 52
ādhāra-kāraṇa 89, 92
adhiṣṭhāna 15
adhikaraṇa(s) 2, 4, 13, 96-97, 104-05
adhyāsa 33
Advaita 2, 36, 53, 76, 81-82
Advaita-brahmasiddhi 23-24, 63
Advaitasiddhi 23-24
Advaitavāda 31
Advaitins 15, 25, 29, 46, 81-82, 84, 88
aham ajñaḥ 54
ahambuddhi 75
ahantāviśiṣṭaṁ caitanyam 55
ahaṁkāra 33
aikya 10
ajñāna-nivṛtti 23-24
Alexander, Samuel 65
all-pervading Consciousness 39
Amalānanda 60
ānanda 3, 29
Ānandabodhācārya 23
Ānandagiri 72
Ānandamayādhikaraṇa 3, 7
Ānandapūrṇa 27
ananya 98
ananyatvam 98
Anekajīvavāda 61
anirvacanīya 14, 23, 82
Anirvacanīyavāda 26
antaḥkaraṇa 36, 75

anupapattis 30
anyonyāśraya 56
aparā-śakti 101
aphorism of Bādarāyaṇa 85
Appaya Dīkṣita 17, 23, 60, 64-65, 67, 69-70, 74
apracyutasvarūpa 86
apṛthaksiddhi 11-12
asahāya 98
asamavāyī 92
Ātman 24
Auḍulomi 68, 70
authoritativeness of Vedas 14
Avantisundarīkathā 8
āvaraṇa-śakti 16
avidyā 32, 34, 38, 51, 54, 56-57, 59, 101
  nature of 45
  should be regarded as the effect of *jīva*-cum-*māyā* 58
  veiling power of 31
avidyā-nivṛtti 23-24
Avimuktātma-Bhagavān 23
avyakta 99

Bādarāyaṇa 2-3, 5, 12, 16, 53-54, 67-68, 70, 72, 104-05
  aphorism of 85
Baladeva 99, 102
Being, Essence of 23, 25
Berkeley, George 59
Bhartṛhari, philosophy of 31
Bhāṣya 11
Bhāgavata Purāṇa 2
Bhāmatī 6, 17, 22, 34, 51, 53-54, 59
Bhartṛhari 30-31
Bhāskara 1, 8, 17-20, 22, 82-85, 87-88, 92, 102-03
Bhāskara Bhāṣya 1
Bhaṭṭa, Jayanta 31
Bhaṭṭa, Nāgeśa 32
Bhāvādvaita doctrine 23
bheda 17, 21
Bhedābheda 2, 7
Bhikṣu 90-91, 93-94, 98, 104
bhogya 10
bhogya-śakti 83
bhoktṛ 10, 97
bhoktṛ-śakti 83
Bimbacaitanya 48, 65
Bodhāyana 8-9
Bodhāyana–Upavarṣa–Vṛttikāra equation 8
brahma-jñāna 23
Brahman 4-6, 10-17, 24-25, 30-32, 34-36, 41, 48, 50-54, 56-58, 60, 62-63, 69, 71, 75-77, 80-87, 89-90, 92, 96-105
  being *causa materialis* 5
  causality of 57, 59-60, 62-63
  conception of 60
  effect of 57
  identity of 31, 67
  integrity of 86
  qualities of 70
  Śakti of 86
  svarūpalakṣaṇa of 3
  the Absolute 63

Brahman as
a Concrete Principle 11
an efficient and substantive cause 12
identity of the efficient and the material cause 82
illusory cause 22
Universal Cause 7
Brahman is
Absolute Being-Consciousness-Bliss (Saccidānanda) 25
qualified 7
Prakṛti 34
substantive cause 13
Brahman-Māyā 52, 54
Brahmapariṇāmavāda 32
Brahma-Sūtras 1-2, 4-5, 8, 12, 54, 89, 94-95, 97, 99, 103, 105
Brahmasiddhi 23
Bṛhatkathāmañjarī 8

Caitanya 1
Candrakīrti 26
causa efficiens 5
Causal
Background in *Īśvara* 72
Brahman 72
causality of
Brahman 57, 59-60, 62-63
Māyā 63
causa materialis 49, 53
causation, doctrine of 35, 64, 75
central doctrine of Upaniṣads 84
Chāndogya Upaniṣad 77, 84, 98
cit 3, 86
Citsukhī 23-24
Citsukhācārya 24
conception of *Brahman* 60
concept of
material causality 58
material cause 16
conjunct causality of the *jīva-cum-Māyā*, theory of 60
Consciousness
eternal existence of 28
falsity of 28
nature of 76
unity of 37
cosmic Energy 60
criterion of Reality 45

Daṇḍin 8
Das Gupta 40, 48
Devācārya 85-86, 88
difference between
Bhāskara and Śaṅkara 84
Brahman and *jīva* 7
Divine Energy 86
doctrine of
causation 35, 64, 75
illusory causation 76
locative causation 58
Lord's Rulership 104
Māyā 80
Durbalācārya 32
Dvaitādvaita 2

Effected Absolute 72
effect of
Brahman 57

Māyā 57
ego-consciousness, evidence of 32
Ekajīvavāda 61
epistemology of perception 45, 82
Essence of Being 23, 25
eternal existence of Consciousness 28
evidence of ego-consciousness 32
Excluded Middle, law of 19
Experience, God of 19
Existence and Consciousness 80

falsity of
  Consciousness 28
  effects 76
Final
  Emancipation 75
  Release 23, 69, 74
    nature of 67
  Salvation 67
finest fruit of Indian thought 1
finite–infinite nature 52
fundamental laws of thought 19

Gauḍīya school 99-101
Gauḍīya Vaiṣṇava school 1
Ghate 84, 98
God of
  Experience 19
  Patañjali 12
Govindabhāṣya 1, 99
Grammarians 30-31
Great Being, Omnipotence of 77
guṇas 10

Hanumad Bhāṣya 1
Highest
  Absolute 72
  Personal God 72-73
  Salvation 74
Hiraṇyagarbha 71-74
His Cosmic Activities 74
history of Vedānta 60

Idealism of Vācaspati 59
Idealist 45
identity
  of *Brahman* 31, 67
  law of 19
Iṣṭasiddhi 23-24
iṣṭasiddhikāra 23-24
illusory
  causation, doctrine of 76
  cause of the world-appearance 77
Impersonal Absolute 60, 64-65
Indian
  philosophy 99
  thought, finest fruit of 1
Indradatta 8
insentience of
  Māyā 35
  world 51, 53
integrity of *Brahman* 86
Īśvara 11, 50, 60-61, 64, 69, 73-74, 94, 98-100
  Causal Background in 72

Īśvarahood 67, 69, 71

jaḍa 35
jaḍatā 50, 52
jaḍatvanirukti 80
jagadabhinnanimittopādāna 105
Jaimini 68-70
Jaina works 28
jīva 54-55, 60-61, 68, 97, 99-100
jñātatā 42
Joy 29, 80
Joy-Existence-Consciousness 77

kālātyayāpadiṣṭa hetu 47
Kalpataru 56, 60-62
kalpita 17
Kant 71
Kapila 10, 93-94
Kāpilas 11
kāraṇarūpā 51
kāraṇa Brahman 72
kartṛtva 33
kārya Brahman 72
Kathāsaritsāgara 8
Kātyāyana 8
Kṣemendra 8
Kṣetrajñaśakti 101
kṣobha 86
Keśava Kāśmīrin 85, 86
Khaṇḍanakhaṇḍakhādya 27
kṛtakoṭi 8
Kuñjikā 32
Kumārila 83

law of
  Excluded Middle 19
  Identity 19
laya 5
logical see-saw 57
Lord
  Buddha 29
  Viṣṇu 99
Mādhava 31, 48
Madhva 1-2, 14, 88, 98-100, 102-03
Mādhva school 99-100
Madhya Bhāṣya 1
Mādhyamika-Kārikās 21-22, 29
Mādhyamikaśāstra 23
Mādhyamikas 22-25, 27, 29-30
Mahopaniṣad 24
Mīmāṁsakas 93-94
Mīmāṁsists 42
Māṇḍūkya Upaniṣad 14
many souls, theory of 61
material causality, concept of 58
material cause
  concept of 16
  reality of 76
Māyā 15-16, 20, 34-36, 38, 41, 45, 47-54, 56-57, 62, 70-71, 74, 80-82
  causality of 63
  effect of 57
  insentience of 35
  is always located in pure self-luminous Consciousness 49
Māyā-śabalam 49
māyā-śakti 82, 101

Miśra, Maṇḍana 11, 23-24
mithyā 14, 82
mithyātva 26
mokṣa 23
Monism of Śaṅkara 26
Monistic
  doctrine 2
  Vedānta 40, 60
Monists 81, 84, 87
Muktāvalī 63, 81

Nāgārjuna 21-22, 25-26, 29
Naiyāyikas 13, 41
nature of
  avidyā 45
  Consciousness 76
  Final Release 67
  Absolute 20
na-vilakṣaṇatva adhikaraṇa 53
nescience, veiling power of 30
Nimbārka 1, 85, 87-89, 102-03
nimitta 5, 14, 92
Nirguṇa-Brahman 64
nirupādhika 33
nirvikāra 86
Non-Being or Darkness 80
Nyāyamañjarī 31

Omnipotence of Great Being 77
Omniscience of Godhood 67
One Concrete Whole 10
One-without-a-Second 23
original Consciousness is Pure Absolute 49

pāda 99
Padārthatattvanirṇaya 35, 47-48, 52
padārthatattvanirṇayakāra 48
Pañcadaśī 59
pāramārthika-sattā 22
Pāṇini 8, 77
Pāṇinian school of Grammarians 30
paramārtha satya 29
pāramārthika 61
Parā Śakti 101
pariṇāma 84
Pariṇāmavāda 32, 84
pariṇāmopādāna 15, 34, 47, 91
Pāśupata Śaivas 2, 12, 103
Pāśupatas 12-13, 99
Pātañjalas 12-13
Patañjali 11
  God of 12
perception, psychology of 36
Personal Deity 66
Personal God 48-49, 56, 60-61, 64, 66, 93-94
  present Rulership of 65
Personal Godhead 71, 73-74
personalised *Brahman* 60
philosophy of
  Bhartṛhari 31
  sphoṭa 31
  Vedānta 6
  Vedāntic Monism 80
positivistic Absolutism 25
Prābhākaras 42

Pradhāna 10, 95-96, 102
Prakāśātman Akhaṇḍānanda 48
prakāra 10
prakārin 10
Prakṛti 10-12, 15, 22, 81-83, 86, 90, 95-96, 99-100
  is body of the changeless *Brahman* 83
pramāṇa 40
pramāṇacaitanya 38
pramātṛcaitanya 37-38
prameyacaitanya 37
pratīti 45
prātibhāsika 61
prātibhāsika-sattā 22
pratibimba 48
pratibimbacaitanya 48
prauḍhivāda 94
preritṛ 10
present Rulership of Personal God 65
Primordial Matter 90
principle of Relativity 24
psychology of perception 36
pṛthivītanmātra 92
Puṇyarāja 31
Pure Absolute
  Consciousness 52
  original Consciousness is 49
Pure
  Brahman 102-03
  Consciousness 30, 32-33, 37, 46, 48-50, 55, 61, 66-69, 80, 82
  Eternal Consciousness 83
  transcendental Consciousness 38
  Unqualified Consciousness 67
pūrvapakṣa 96

qualified
  Brahman 69
  Monism 14, 54
qualities of *Brahman* 70

Radhakrishnan, S. 8, 10, 16-17, 52, 78, 86
rajas 10
Rāmānuja 1, 7-8, 10-12, 14, 30, 46, 53, 69-71, 75, 81-83, 87-89, 102-03
Ratnaprabhā 7
real transformation of *Brahman*, theory of 32
Reality
  criterion of 45
  of material cause 76
relation of *Brahman* and *Prakṛti* 91
Revealed Text 84
Ṛgveda 78, 98

Śabda-Brahman 30, 32
Śabdabrahmavāda 31
saguṇa-Brahman 7
Saguṇa-Brahmopāsanā 67
sahakāri 51
Śaiva
  Liṅgāyat school 12
  Viśiṣṭādvaita 1
Śaivādvaita philosophy 65

sākṣicaitanya 46
Śakti of *Brahman* 86
śaktivikṣepalakṣaṇapariṇāma 86
salakṣaṇa 13
Śālikanātha 42
samavāya 91
samavāyī 92
Sāṁkhya 40-41, 93-94, 96
system 32, 93-94, 96
Sāṁkhya-Sūtras 89
Sāṁkhya–Yoga
system 93, 95, 97
theories 95
Sāṁkhyapravacanabhāṣya 89
Sāṁkhyas 10-11, 13, 32, 53, 86, 93-94, 102
Saṁkṣepaśārīraka 48-50, 54
Samuel Alexander, theory of 64
sāṁvṛta 29
satya 29
Śaṅkara 1-4, 7, 11-12, 20-21, 26, 67, 69, 71, 73-74, 80, 82, 84-85, 92, 103, 105
Monism of 26
Śāṅkara Bhāṣya 6
Śāṅkara Vedānta 34, 57
Sarasvatī, Madhusūdana 24
śarīra 10
Sarvadarśanasaṁgraha 23, 25, 34
Sarvārthasiddhi 22
Śāstras 80
Śāstrī, A.K. 15, 34
Śāstrī, Kuppusvāmī 8
Śāstrī, Mahāmahopādhyāya
Anantakṛṣṇa 8
sat 3, 35
Ṣaṭsandarbha 1
sattātraividhya-vāda 22
sattva 10
Scared Revelation 37
self-evolution of matter 11
Self-luminous Pure Consciousness 41
Siddāntamuktāvalī 82
Siddhāntabindu 49
Siddhāntaleśasaṁgraha 17, 23, 52, 60, 64
Siddhāntamuktāvalī 62-63, 81
simultaneous difference and non-difference, theory of 22
Śivādvaitanirṇaya 65
Ślokavārttika 83
Smṛtis 93
Sogen, Yamakami 23-26
Solipsism 58
Somadeva 8
sopādhika 33
sphoṭa 31
philosophy of 31
theory of 30
Sphoṭasiddhi 11
Spiritual Illumination 71, 74
Śrī Puruṣottama 86
Śrīdhara 2
Śrīharṣa 26, 27
Śrīkaṇṭha 1, 103
Śrīkara Bhāṣya 12

Śrīnivāsācārya 85
Śruti 83-86, 92, 97-98, 100-03, 105
stages of emancipation 71
Stcherbatsky, Th. 23, 25-26
sthiti 5
Subjective Idealism 59-60
Subjectivism 58, 61
subject–object relation 41-45
Śuddhabrahmapariṇāmavāda 103
Śuddhacaitanya 36
Śuddhādvaita 2, 102
śūnya 22-24, 28, 30, 99
śūnyatā 25
Śūnyavāda 26-27
super-subtle Word-Essence 30
Supreme
  Being 2, 86
  Creator *Īśvara* 71
  Illumination 67
  Knowledge 73
  Omniscience 77
  Salvation 73
Supremest
  Form of Emancipation 75
  State of Salvation 74
Sureśvara 63, 81
sūtrakāra 93, 104
svābhāvika 87
svādhiṣṭhāna-caitanya 38
svaprakāśa 28, 36
svarūpabheda 10
svarūpalakṣaṇa 80
  of *Brahman* 3
svarūpapariṇāma 85
svatantrasattva 89

Tadananyatva 97
tadananyatvam 98
Taittirīya Brāhmaṇa 78
tamas 10, 80
tanmātra 91
tattantrasattva 89
Tattvadīpana 34
Ṭhākura, Bilvamaṅgala 2
The Bhāmatī Catussūtrī 65
theory of
  Abhinnanimittopādāna 97
  conjunct causality of the *jīva*-cum-*Māyā* 60
  many souls 61
  real transformation of *Brahman* 32
  Samuel Alexander 64
  simultaneous difference and non-difference 22
  sphoṭa 30
  transformation of *Brahman* 85
  vṛtti 40
Thibaut Georg Wilhelm Friedrich 70, 84
thought, fundamental laws of 19
threefold energies 102
Transcendental
  Absolute 64-65, 67
  Entity 64
transformation of *Brahman*, theory of 85

twofold *upādāna* 36

uccheda 84
Udayana 26
Ultimate
  Consciousness 36
  Impersonal Absolute 60
  Reality 22, 28-29, 36, 47, 77
  Release 71, 75
  Salvation 73
unity of Consciousness 37
Universal
  Causation 7
  Cause 4, 76-77
Unqualified
  Brahman 74
  Consciousness 55
upādāna 5, 10-12, 14, 36, 91, 101
upādānatā 6, 35, 58
upādhis 66, 87
upalakṣaṇa 50
Upaniṣads 1-3, 31, 66, 72, 76-77, 105
  central doctrine of 84
Upavarṣa 8-9, 82-83

Vācaspati 6, 12, 17, 22, 26, 34, 51-64
  Idealism of 59
Vaiśeṣikas 13, 18, 92-93
Vaiyākaraṇasiddhāntamañjūṣā 32
Vākyapadīya 30-31
Vallabha 2, 102-04
Varṣa 8
Vārttika 81-82
vāsanā(s) 51, 59
Vāsanā Bhāṣya 1
Vedānta 1, 4-5, 7, 28, 37, 40, 52, 58, 71, 86, 93, 95, 105
  Absolute of 29
  history of 60
  philosophy 6, 18, 58
  system 95
Vedāntadeśika 8
Vedāntakaustubhaprabhā 85
Vedāntaparibhāṣā 15
Vedānta-Sūtras 95
Vedāntic
  Absolutism 27
  Monism 31, 54
    philosophy of 80
  Monists 20-21, 30
  writers 36
Vedāntist 45
Vedas 20, 77, 98
vedaprāmāṇya 14
Vedic
  Saṁhitās 78
  speculations 80
veiling power of
  avidyā 31
  nescience 30
vidyā 24
Vidyābhūṣaṇa, Baladeva 1
Vidyāraṇya 26, 28
Vidyāsāgarī 27
Viśiṣṭādvaitavāda 14
Viṣṇu 2, 99
Viṣṇuśakti 101
Viṣṇu Purāṇa 101

Viṣṇusvāmin 2
Vijñānabhikṣu 2, 12, 58, 81, 89, 92, 95-96, 99, 103
Vijñānāmṛtabhāṣya 89
vikṣepaśakti 10, 16
vilakṣaṇa 13
vilakṣaṇatva 13
viśeṣaṇa 10
viśiṣṭa 89
Viśiṣṭādvaita 2, 12, 82
Vivaraṇa 34, 48, 50, 54-56, 60-61, 65
vivaraṇakāra 48
Vivaraṇaprameyasaṁgraha 55
vivartopādāna 15-16, 22, 34, 36, 47, 82
vivartta theory 29
Vivarttavāda 6, 31-32
vṛtti 8, 36, 38-39, 80
  theory of 40
    perception 40
vṛtticaitanya 38
vṛttijñāna 46
vṛttikāra Bodhāyana 7
Vyāḍi 8
vyāpaka 87
Vyāsa 12
vyāvahārika 17, 61
vyāvahārika-sattā 22

world, insentience of 51, 53

Yoga 93
  philosophy 11
  Śāstra 11
  system 95
Yogasvarodaya Brāhmaṇa 24